Making POLICY

Making CHANGE

How Communities Are Taking
Law into Their Own Hands

Makani N. Themba

**Chardon
Press**
Berkeley, CA

To my mother Ananda Sattwa for the wisdom,
wondering and wings that made me who I am.

Library of Congress Catalog Card Number: 99-74604
ISBN 1-890759-07-4

Cover and book design by Cici Kinsman, C² Graphics, Oakland, CA
Editing by Nancy Adess

Printed in the United States of America.
Printed on recycled paper.

A Chardon Press–Applied Research Center collaboration.

Chardon Press
3781 Broadway
Oakland, California 94611
(510) 596-8160
www.chardonpress.com

10 9 8 7 6 5 4 3 2 1

Front cover photo: Makani N. Themba
*Community coalitions gather to support local control of alcohol outlets
at California's State Capitol (October, 1993).*

Author photo, back cover: Frankie Frost

Contents

Foreword

This is a deceptive book; it is a subversive book. But if you think I mean ill of those adjectives, think again. Makani Themba is deceptive herein because her guidance to community leaders and activists seeking social change is direct, clear, practical, tested—and deceptively simple.

In this book, Makani has distilled clarity out of jumble; teased the practical out of the theoretical; distilled the essence of hard-won experience out of the turmoil of campaigning. This work is not simple. The lessons are not obvious. No one has done anything quite like this before. Yet the social activist seeking guidance will find a clear road map from anger and frustration with city hall to strategic activism to effective social change. This is an extraordinary achievement.

Makani achieves this through subversion: She subverts all the categories and divisions into which we lazily pigeonhole political activists and community activism. Is she a radical? You bet—in her passion for root and branch social change, and in drawing upon the analytical traditions and insights of Marx and Mao.

Is she a conservative? Absolutely, invoking the spiritual power of the community-centered church and the moral force of prophetic language.

Is she a dreaded liberal? Of course, seeing and seizing the possibilities of tangible progress through full-throated participation in electoral and legislative process, which most radicals disdain—though her focus is the potential of local government, where our political institutions remain in reach to those citizens who take the time to understand how to make their representatives pay heed.

Like our own Old Testament prophet, Ralph Nader, does she view unaccountable corporate hegemony of our lives as the deepest threat to our democratic polis? Does she believe that our mass media are a pillar of the corporate establishment and, hence, skewered toward the preservation of the status quo? She does. Yet she proceeds to instruct us shrewdly in strategic, effective techniques for getting our stories told our way, and in making the media a hammer in our toolkit of change agents.

Is she a civil rights advocate? A civil libertarian? An advocate for dreaded government regulation? A public health advocate? A consumer advocate? A feminist advocate? What the tobacco and alcohol and gun industries would call a "health Nazi?"

All of the above.

And you, the reader, are the beneficiary. For *Making Policy, Making Change* draws the wisest and most practical lessons and counsel from all these movements and disciplines. Some of us learn best by straightforward, step-by-step guidance. Here, you have it. Others learn best by example. Here, in the case studies, in which Makani modestly plays down her own sparkplug role, she gives us amazing stories of communities aroused, strategic, and winning—against some of the most potent opposition corporate America can mount. From them, we both learn and are inspired.

And she talks straight to us about the internal conflicts and challenges that can plague even the most honorable movements and campaigns, and ways of coping and overcoming them.

She inspires as she teaches. What could be more subversive than that!

Mike Pertschuk
Co-director, Advocacy Institute

Acknowledgments

Like most things women do, this book was written between dinner dishes, meetings, child crises and, well, just plain life. At one point, the stress of getting this done on time weighed so heavy on my person that I was breaking out in rashes But, hey, it's here! An exclamation that would not be possible without the following wonderful people: Gary Delgado for the constant inspiration, feedback, wisdom and money that made this possible; Mike Pertschuk for the support, ears and money that helped to keep me afloat while I wrote; Evangeline Koch and the crew at the American Leadership Forum for an incredible learning opportunity through my work with the Collaborative Leadership in Action initiative; Omowale Satterwhite for just being Omowale, which is a synonym for all things good and nurturing; and my honorary "dad," Greg Akili, for his principled struggle with me on my work throughout a big part of my life. Much of what's here started with you.

I am also indebted to the many activists who shared their stories with me throughout this process, including Councilwoman Alberta Tinsley Williams in Detroit; Karen Bass, Sylvia Castillo, Solomon Rivera and Marqueece Dawson of the Community Coalition; State Representative Johnnie Morris-Tatum, Ann Wilson, Betty Glosson, James White, Terrance Herron, Talibah Mateen, Dalvery Wilbourn and Hasheem Shabazz in Milwaukee; Bev Thomas and Kevin Jordan in Baltimore; Karen Gaffney in Eugene; Glenn Wierenga, Mary Darling and Jill Anne Yeagley in New Mexico; Tom Hudson and Frank Johnson in Unionville; the "most dear" Taj James, Colleen Floyd-Carroll, Rev. Alpha Brown, Beverly Watts-Davis, Mark Pertschuk, Rebecca Gordon, and Van Jones.

Adam Glickman of the New Party, Jenn Kern of ACORN, the brilliant and insightful Dr. Maria Alaniz, Rosalinda "the visionary" Palacios, Amos White, Greg Hodge, Paul Orum of Community Right To Know, Cynthia Valencic of LEAF, Katie Woodruff of Berkeley Media Studies

Group; Eris Weaver at the Marin Institute; Diane Jones, Julia Carroll, Robin Hobart and Elva Yanez of Americans for Nonsmokers' Rights all contributed important information to the case study section—thank you for your time, wisdom and generosity. Thanks are also due to The Marin Institute for the Prevention of Alcohol and Other Drug Problems for providing an intellectual home to me for five years during which this project began to germinate—most especially my colleagues in the Center for Media and Policy Analysis, Pam Glenn, Hilary Abramson, Alison Seevak, Rose Works, Melissa Magallanes, Humberto Cintron and Bob Kadoyama. And finally, thanks to Mandrake and Paul Kelly who are no longer physically with us but whose work and wisdom continues to inspire so many long after their untimely deaths. As they say in the islands, remember we.

The case study on the Baltimore Citywide Liquor Coalition in Chapter 2 is an abridged version of a longer piece by Alison Seevak titled, "Tapping the Hearts and Minds of Everyday People," written for the Marin Institute. The case study on the Louisiana Coalition for Tax Justice in Chapter 3 was written by Ron Nixon and Akilah Monifa. The section on base building in Chapter 4 drew heavily from materials and lectures by organizer and teacher extraordinaire Greg Akili. Finally, the section on media advocacy in Chapter 5 includes a great deal of the terms, framework and materials of the Berkeley Media Studies Group, undoubtedly the leading institution advancing the notion of media advocacy and a group of people with whom I'm proud to collaborate on occassion. I'm indebted to all of these folk for their contributions to this book. All are used here by permission.

Special thanks to my dear colleagues and friends who listened to me go on and on about the concepts in this book, and who critiqued them and offered invaluable insights, especially Lori Dorfman, Larry Wallack, Thandi and Mahmood Hicks-Harper (one love!), Esther Iverem, Vivian Chavez, Denise Herd, Tyler Stovall, Robert Robinson, Elva Yanez, Robin Hobart, my cyber family at blackpower, my sistah Ann Jefferson, Minister Keith Brown, Ann Wilson, Clarence Lusane, David Cohen, Joani Marinoff, Jennifer Logan, Amy Hill, Colleen Floyd Carroll, Taj James, Lisa Sullivan, Roberta Ponce, Karolyn Tyson, Kim Deterline & Hunter Cutting of the innovative and highly effective group, We Interrupt This Message, Marianne Manilov, Nancy Nadel, Phil Hutchings, Cassandra Youngblood and Tamu Jones. Jan Adams at ARC and the staff at Chardon Press deserve special thanks for their efforts to "keep things moving forward" on the arduous road from idea to finished product. A very special thanks to my editor, Nancy Adess, whose thorough and thoughtful comments improved this book a great deal.

Warm thanks are due to *all* of my colleagues at the Grass Roots Innovative Policy Program and Applied Research Center for their support and feedback on these concepts, especially Janene Wiley, Lauren Wiley, Rose-May Guignard, Jan Adams, Jeff Chang, Bob Wing, Terry Keleher, Gavin Kearney, John Beam, Libero Della Piana, Rebecca Gordon, Francis Calpotura, LeeAnn Hall, Deepak Bhargava, Ludovic Blaine and the folks at each of the local sites kicking serious booty for the movement, including BOSS Community Organizing Team, People United for A Better Oakland, Idaho Community Action Network, Indian People's Action, Metropolitan Alliance of Congregations, South Carolina Fair Share, People Organized for Work and Employment Rights and The Coalition for Quality Education. Thanks also to the folk at the Kopkind Colony for the engaging discussion and idyllic surroundings that really helped me complete this project.

Thanks are due, too, to George Clinton, W.E.B. DuBois, Terry Gilliam, Alice Walker, Don Byron, Star Trek (all generations), John Coltrane, Joni Mitchell, The Coup, Dianne Reeves and Chaka Khan for providing a great deal of artistic inspiration for this project. And of course, I must also extend warm thanks and appreciation to my "biological" family who provide me with love, support, intellectual stimulation—and low-cost entertainment. My brother Robin D.G. Kelley for his encouragement and support and thoughtful contributions to the book and to my growth throughout my life. To my sisters, Fujiko Kelley, Diedra Harris Kelley and Meilan Carter for being there, listening and making me laugh. My brother Chris Kelley for believing. My niece Elleza and my nephews Kamau and Brandon for just being you. My grandmothers, Carmen Chambers and Aileen Kelley, whom I quote in many meetings and speeches—thanks for the common sense, love and faith. To my children, Miles, Laura, Marketta and Ronnie, who contributed their ideas and put up with many days without me— yes, mommy's done with the book now! My mother, Ananda Sattwa, who took care of my kids while trying to handle midterms, term papers and the like: there are no words to express my love and appreciation for your support. You and grandma always said I had a book in me. Hope you like it. My "other mother" Lillie B. Nixon for giving me your son, love, and encouragement. Finally, a big Jacques Cousteau-Jules

Verne-aqua boogie thanks to my husband, my love and partner, Ron Nixon (is that deep enough?) for the criticism, the editing, the contributions, the ideas, the ears, the distraction—especially the distraction—and the support. This couldn't have happened without you.

There are numerous others deserving of thanks that I had not room to name. Thank you all for your support and insight.

This book is a product of love and blessings so I must close by giving much props to the One who makes all things possible. To all of these folk go the credit but none of the blame. The mistakes and shortcomings that may appear within these pages are mine alone.

Peace and blessings,
Makani N. Themba

Introduction

Well, after I saw this fool on television, talking about our neighborhood,
it got me to thinking: That man is my councilman and he's supposed
to represent me. He doesn't know anything about what's going on
here. I best be getting down to City Hall and give him some direction.

—MRS. E. JOHNSON, OAKLAND, CALIFORNIA NEIGHBORHOOD ACTIVIST [1]

In 1993, I found myself sitting in a church basement where a meeting of the Baltimore Citywide Liquor Coalition for Better Rules and
Regulation was taking place. The meeting started with a prayer, solemn
and long, Baptist-style, as the host minister asked for God's blessing on
every aspect of their effort. He prayed especially for God to speak personally with the legislators they were about to approach in their efforts
to rid Baltimore of alcohol and tobacco billboards.

Yes, he was praying for the legislators.

I couldn't help but notice that the people in the group, comprised
mostly of African-American seniors, were not much different than my
own grandparents. They were kind, spiritual people who had put down
roots in this community and were willing to fight City Hall, or whomev-
er, to make it safer for themselves and their families. What distinguished
them was how they were fighting. Instead of simply reacting to policymakers in a defensive mode, they had gone on the offensive and were
approaching legislators with their own carefully drawn legislation.

Policy development, previously the domain of expert "wonks" and
lobbyists, is increasingly being used as a tool for community change.
Grassroots groups are taking their own agendas to City Hall and the State
House and transforming them into progressive, meaningful policies.

- More than 600 local policies have been passed to regulate tobacco
  availability, use and marketing. Local coalitions have taken the

leadership by writing ordinances that best address local problems and organizing broad support.[2]

- Nearly 100 gun control and violence-prevention policies have been enacted since 1991, about half of those in California alone.[3]
- Milwaukee, Boston and Oakland are among the cities that have passed Living-Wage ordinances, local laws that guarantee higher than minimum wages for workers (usually set as the minimum needed to keep a family of four above poverty).[4]

These are just a few examples of local policy advocacy making inroads where national policy was stonewalled. Increasingly, the local policy arena is where the action is and where activists are finding (relatively) the least resistance. Of course, corporate interests—which are usually the target of these policies—are gearing up in defense. Their tactics include front groups, economic pressure and the tried-and-true—cold, hard cash.

Grassroots groups prevail in the face of these barriers in large part because grassroots organizing is most effective at the smaller scale of local politics and has greater access to elected officials, and because of officials' greater reliance on their constituents for re-election. For example, getting 400 people to City Hall in just about any city in the U.S. is quite impressive. Four hundred people have much less impact, however, at the State House and less still at the House of Representatives. Add to that the fact that all 400 people at City Hall are usually constituents of the lawmakers within, and the impact is even greater.

IT'S WORTH GETTING IT IN WRITING

Simple and faithless as a smile and shake of the hand.

—T. S. ELIOT, *LA FIGLIA CHE PIANGE*[5]

Too many activists are content to negotiate agreements with powerful interests without getting those agreements codified as law. After all the organizing, media work and effort, a group should leave a decision-maker they've targeted with more than a handshake and his or her word. Activists resist getting agreements translated into written policies because to do so means maneuvering through the bureaucracy and dealing with its technical language, and overcoming the all-too-common resistance of decisionmakers to take the next step. Still, if it's worth organizing for, it's worth having in writing—whether as law, regulation or internal policy.

Policy is more than law. It is any agreement (formal or informal) on how an institution, governing body or community will address shared problems or attain shared goals. It spells out the terms and the consequences of these agreements and is the codification of the body's values—as represented by those present in the policymaking process. Given who's usually present, most policies reflect the political agenda of the powerful and, as described in Chapter 1, are usually concerned with the support and protection of private enterprise.

Yet, policy can be a force for change. Good policies can affect a community in at least two ways. First, the policy itself, when enacted, can address problems that put communities at risk for crime, drug use, poverty, etc., and help improve quality of life. For example, policies to reduce access to tobacco have resulted in decreased tobacco use and tobacco-related deaths. Successful campaigns to raise local wages and improve worker benefits have meant, among other things, increased access to health care and stabilized nutrition for affected families.

Second, the act of organizing a community to engage in a policy initiative can be as effective in reducing problems as the policy itself. Voluntary participation in local community institutions and organizations has long been considered vital for effective crime and drug abuse prevention.[6] Efforts that engage community residents and give them a sense of their own power enhance a community's ability to solve problems and strengthen individual members' sense of "community."[7] Lack of a sense of community, or "neighborhood disorganization," is considered a critical risk factor for crime and drug problems.[8] Community-based efforts to change policy not only address problems through the policy changes they achieve, but they also aid communities in confronting the factors that put them at risk in the first place.

The best kind of policy initiative engages the community that shares the problem and ensures it is a part of the solution. These initiatives match the desired policy with the capacity of the community to advocate for change, while seeking to expand the base of support for such advocacy efforts in the future.

WORKING BELOW THE RADAR

Much of this work has been ignored by scholars, funders and even other activists. Too often, progressives mourn that "we have too few victories" while ignoring the groundswell of community action. Yes, many of these groups don't look like the "typical activist" organization. They don't often use timeworn, progressive buzzwords like "organizing" or "activism" when describing their work. And some who lead this work are, in some ways, really quite conservative, ideologically speaking.

However, despite this obscurity, work in the local policy arena has been the most vital expression of "people-centered" politics in recent history. The most far-reaching policies dealing with corporate account-ability, public health and environmental protection have all emerged from the local arena. And the most diverse coalitions on these issues have formed at the local level. National organizations seeking social change have often failed to attract participation beyond the usual poli-cy wonks or other advocacy groups remarkably similar to their own. Local coalitions working on the same issues often attract more activists from communities of color, and forge broad alliances and non-tradi-tional partnerships.

In alcohol policy, for example, national coalitions to reduce youth access to alcohol have consisted mostly of predominantly white organi-zations focussing on alcohol prevention. Many local coalitions, on the other hand, working on the same issues, engaged organizations work-ing for racial justice, trade unions and concerned merchants along with traditional public health allies. National coalitions did, in fact, become more diverse as a result of contact with local coalition partners. These partners helped to attract the support of new national groups, which in turn helped to further catalyze diversity in the field.

LOOKING BEYOND THE BELTWAY

Given the many contributions of local policy development, why have funders and scholars (outside of public health) pretty much ignored this phenomenon? Much of the problem lies in their narrow focus on Washington, D.C. Policy has become synonymous with feder-al politics. The national agenda is considered to be confined to the events unfolding on the congressional stage.

Historically, the genesis of policy analysis organizations (or think tanks) was to inform and influence federal policy. It was clear by the early 1900s that the work of policymaking was becoming increasingly complex. Policy organizations emerged both within and outside of gov-ernment to help fill the growing need for information and analysis. Large-scale institutions were founded with the support of wealthy patrons like Andrew Carnegie (Carnegie Endowment for International Peace), Margaret Olivia Sage (Russell Sage Foundation), and Edward A. Filene (The Twentieth Century Fund). By the end of the World War II, hundreds of millions of dollars were being invested in these and similar institutions annually—mostly in hopes of generating public policy in support of the various interests that funded these organizations.[9]

As corporations gained power and prominence during the 1920s, they approached public policy with increasing sophistication and resources. Policies that supported business deregulation, corporate tax relief and reduced social programs flourished. The Depression and World War II brought more attention to the need for social programs and stemmed this trend temporarily, enabling think tanks focusing on child welfare and employment policies to play a larger role in policymaking. However, it was clear that business interests dominated most of the policy discourse by assembling a formidable intellectual network, which controlled research at think tanks and at most academic institutions.

With such an infrastructure in place, social programs and initiatives were thoroughly scrutinized by the corporate academic community. The singular question became, "Is this good for business?" It took the massive civil unrest of the 1960s to wrest away some of the influence of these institutions over public policy. In light of the Civil Rights Movement, organizations dealing with social welfare issues played a role once more in developing proposals to address systemic poverty, unemployment and racism.

Known mostly as the War on Poverty, these initiatives were crafted as large-scale, social-change endeavors designed to fund and support civic and programmatic infrastructure in communities that were most affected by poverty and racism. The programs built on Franklin Roosevelt-era neighborhood-development initiatives, work programs, and grassroots organizing by local groups to launch what Lyndon Johnson called "the great experiment."

Prior to the War on Poverty, business-oriented policy institutions focused narrowly on business regulation and related policies and mainly argued against social policies because they directly affected business interests. Social policy organizations focused mostly on developing information and proposals that dealt with family welfare and social services. This changed as business-oriented policy organizations decided to take on the War on Poverty as a way to fight for reduced social spending and win lower tax rates for corporations. Instead of arguing that the War on Poverty was bad for business as they might have done previously, these organizations pronounced the initiative ineffective and claimed it hurt the people it proposed to help by impeding job creation and creating dependency. This strategy set a trend for the way conservative think tanks would operate for the next 30 years.

Policy organizations like the American Enterprise Institute and the Heritage Foundation—funded by and focused on corporations—increasingly controlled public debate on a wider and wider range of issues through the skillful use of in-house analytical and opinion research and through high-profile dissemination of their message. Older, more "liberal" policy organizations were increasingly edged out of the debate. Some, like the Brookings Institution, were the target of negative media campaigns by their newer, more conservative colleagues and as a result were rendered less effective at countering many of these policy initiatives.

By the 1980s, funders concerned about the rightward shift in federal policy regarding families and corporate accountability began to invest more money in policy analysis on the national level. Organizations like the Center on Budget and Policy Priorities and the Center for Law and Social Policy emerged during this period to provide policy analysis supporting the interests of low-income people—and to provide a counterpoint to more conservative forces.[10]

As a result, much recent progressive policy work has focused on Capitol Hill in an all-out effort to maintain ground, much less advance anything new. Work outside of the Beltway has consisted largely of D.C.-based national groups contacting local activists to garner opposition or support, as legislation required. The little victories that have been won, though important, have rarely been the stuff to get people out into the streets. Even such far-ranging policies as the repeal of welfare in 1997 was difficult for national organizations to translate into local action beyond letter writing and calling officials to protest. Much of the political action coordinated by these groups emphasized marches as a show of strength in (where else?) Washington, D.C.

It has become apparent to progressives that work at the federal level cannot exist without a vital, local base of support and partnership. Some national policy groups have realized the importance of partnering with and supporting local initiatives and that it is no longer realistic (if it ever was) to ask local groups to "fall in line" behind their national strategy without any quid pro quo.

Some of these partnerships have been forged out of necessity. With changes in Congress, it is more difficult for progressive policy institutions to simply state their case and depend on common politics and sympathies to sway public officials. Further, a new Republican majority in Congress has meant new players. Beltway advocacy groups with years of relationships on Capitol Hill have increasingly had to work from scratch to build relationships with new and mostly hostile officials. To leverage more influence, these groups have sought partners among these new representatives' local constituents.

Changes at the congressional level have also forced other new strategies. Thanks to the flourishing of local initiatives nationwide, Washington is no longer so influential in setting the policy agenda. Still, funders and scholars invest most of their resources there. Even funding designed to encourage local–national policy partnerships primarily goes to national groups to provide training and technical assistance to local groups. Local–national tensions and funding priorities are discussed in more detail in Chapter 6. However, it is important to note here that local policy work deserves more public attention, not only for its local impact but because it is now the primary form in which social policy is developed.

Progressives should claim, exalt and support those who do this work as part of "the movement," just as conservatives claim anti-abortion organizations, the National Rifle Association and school voucher advocates as part of their "movement." Local policy initiatives are a vast, diverse body of work that draws from core progressive values, including corporate accountability, participatory democracy and social justice. In fact, the history of local policy advocacy was mostly forged by activists trying, as my grandmother often says, "to make a way out of no way" in the tough arena of public policy.

THE BIRTH OF THE NEW LOCALISM

Think globally. Act locally.

Grassroots activism to enact local policy is not new. Well-heeled suburbanites have engaged in the policy arena for years—especially over issues of land use and zoning. It's not uncommon for a gated or "planned" community to retain a lawyer for the sole purpose of working with public officials in its interest. What is new is that those who have long been shut out of the policy process are now vying with public officials for the driver's seat. Of course, this did not happen overnight. This work was bred and nurtured in the 1970s and 1980s when many observers outside the movement had declared progressive political work all but dead.

The local policy movement has its roots in the many community development struggles that blossomed in the late 1960s and early 1970s. Neighborhood groups brought the national struggle for civil rights to the local level by fighting for basic services like quality schools, decent housing and public safety. One important result of their efforts was funding for local social programs and organizations. This created an infrastructure of social change professionals who were able to support more long-term, sophisticated struggles in the policy arena.

Many of these professionals worked in newly funded programs that had "maximum feasible participation" clauses requiring the programs to be administered with input from community residents. Head Start, for example, required that neighborhood parents have seats on policy committees up until 1968. Programs for urban renewal and related "poverty programs" and other redevelopment projects required community representation on governing boards and community notice of meetings of their governing boards. State and local agencies were also made to follow this regulatory trend as departments were required to post public notices of proposed policies in affected neighborhoods.[11]

Another important trend that helped nurture local policy efforts was the relatively large increase in the number of elected officials of color—especially African Americans. The number of black elected officials more than doubled from 1960 to 1970.[12] This greater representation, coupled with more opportunities for participation, spurred activists toward work in the local policy arena. They learned the committee structures, followed the agenda and public notices and organized support when something antithetical to community interests was afoot. With new funding, neighborhood associations were formed or revived from old Roosevelt-era formations—the last time monies were funneled into urban communities on such a large scale.

This work was mostly reactive until the early 1980s, when a resurgence in radical organizing ushered in a new era of local policy activism. This activism was in large part catalyzed by aggressive federal initiatives to cut funds for urban centers. Under the Reagan Administration, cities were stripped of important matching funds, vitiating housing and social service programs, and many sources of local revenue were redirected to state and federal agencies. Meanwhile, suburban voters were galvanized to engage in outright tax rebellion through well-funded, right-wing initiatives. Voters in California and other states approved dramatic cuts in property taxes and other sources of local funding. The result: even further reductions in local revenues. Local activist groups that had long received public support or government contracts found their funding cut back and their organizations fighting for survival. Long-time professional activists were laid off in the fray and forced to find work elsewhere.

The resource drain was devastating. Cities were under attack from all sides and there was no longer much of an activist/agency infrastructure to monitor the trends and mount a counter attack. New organizations took the leadership in these battles. These new players were, for the most part, from an emerging group of left-wing political organizations whose radical analysis and in-your-face tactics attracted large numbers of young people of color (especially those in college) who were fed up with the status quo. Groups like the Communist Workers Party, Line of March and the League of Revolutionary Struggle used graffiti, street theater and traffic disruption to promote their anti-capitalist ideas.

These groups used the teachings of Marx and Mao, among others, to provide a more systemic analysis of urban problems. They fought against South African apartheid and cutbacks in social spending and services. They organized parallel labor unions where traditional trade unions wouldn't organize, and advanced local policy initiatives based on their socialist economic agenda using the local ballot initiative process. Combining radical organizing and electoral politics was a new and powerful notion that inspired activists nationwide. For example, these groups sponsored early ballot initiatives on rent control and divesting local government or institutional investments in apartheid South Africa, which inspired more mainstream activists to mount electoral campaigns to freeze the proliferation of nuclear weaponry and reduce military spending.

These early initiatives built a new cadre of activists who had "cut their teeth" in the electoral arena. This work offered an ideal training ground because it was concrete and focused. It had a timeline, it required discipline and it had a clear objective—all of which made these initiatives easy to replicate. As a result, activists often traveled the country to jump-start electoral initiatives replicating those successful elsewhere. Many in the leadership of these cutting-edge organizations went to work on these initiatives, bringing their expertise and networks with them. Their efforts helped to forge a national network of policy-savvy activists seeking to advance a progressive political agenda.

By the time Jesse Jackson—a Baptist minister and highly visible long-time civil rights advocate—ran for president in 1984, this network was experienced and poised to provide their wholehearted support. While traditional civil rights leaders discouraged Jackson from running for fear of splitting the black vote, radical and progressive activists joined his campaign staff in large numbers and pushed for endorsement of the campaign in their organizational publications. Work in the campaign was considered so important that many of these radical formations all but shut down other organizing campaigns to support Jackson. Perhaps most important, many of these activists were inspired to mount their own campaigns for local office—again raising the number of people of color in local public office, which increased by more than 50 percent between 1983 and 1986.[13]

Work in the electoral arena had such a profound impact on activist groups that a number of them decided as a matter of ideological principle that local policy work was the most critical thing they could do to further their radical political agenda. Many groups even disbanded their national organizations in order to free membership to work exclusively on influencing the political agenda of local government. In addition to running candidates, many activists sought staff work in local government, often to work for newly elected fellow organizers. The result was an increase not only in the number of local elected officials who were progressively minded, but also in the ranks of more sympathetic city staffers who wanted their work to contribute to social change.

All of this helped to open the doors of City Hall to "regular" folk like never before. Activist groups now had more access (but still much less than more affluent interests) and, thanks to their recent history in electoral work, a lot more experience to draw from. All of this set the stage for present-day activism in the local policy arena.

Recent trends in government only underscore the importance of local policy. Congress has enacted a series of measures devolving significant power to state and local government. Welfare, health care, the regulation of food and the safety of drinking water are among the areas where state and localities have greater rule.

Devolution has some negative consequences, to be sure. History has taught us that, for social services and civil rights in particular, the lack of clear federal standards and mechanisms for accountability lead to uneven and even discriminatory implementation of policies with harmful effects. Still, there are real opportunities for advancing progressive initiatives in this more localized environment. Greater local control can mean greater community power to shape and implement important social policies that were heretofore out of reach. It will require careful attention to the mechanics of local policymaking and a clear blueprint of what we are for.

WHERE I ENTER

The work described above has been a big part of my life in some shape or form for nearly two decades. Like many of my colleagues, I started in a radical political organization as an organizer and took the experience I garnered to a variety of progressive activities: the Jackson campaign; a local initiative to address military spending; and then much further afield to staff positions for a city councilman and a state legislator. This book is as much a chronicle of the work of organizing for local policy advocacy as it is a guide to how to do it, a gathering of the wisdom some of us have earned the hard way so that those who wish to replicate this work will replicate the best of it—or, at least, make new mistakes.

And let me make this clear. The stories in this book belong to those who shared them with me and their inclusion in this book is in no way any attempt to take credit for this work. The credit belongs to the activists who undertook these campaigns and I am greatly appreciative for their willingness to share their insights. I hope the breadth and diversity of these stories will inspire others to undertake similar campaigns; help funders to see the importance and wisdom of investing in this work; and prod all of us who do this work to look past facile labels like labor organizing, public health advocacy, child advocacy, etc., and recognize we are all in one movement with a set of shared values in a vast and wonderful division of labor.

My participation in this field was mostly honed in the public health arena, where literally thousands of local, funded coalitions are called upon to create policies that will affect major health challenges like smoking, alcohol-related problems and illegal drug use. For the past seven years, I've been conducting training and technical assistance for hundreds of these coalitions. I've criss-crossed the country many times watching this process of local policy advocacy unfold in places like Unionville, Georgia; Kearney, Nebraska; and San Bernardino, California. A significant portion of this book is drawn from these trainings and the stories and approaches that came out of exploring issues such as grassroots research, issue definition and media advocacy.

Aside from the case studies, this book focuses on public health coalitions because they are probably the best-funded community advocacy organizations in the country—and the most stringently evaluated. Funding is relative, of course, but in the case of these coalitions, many have staff, offices and equipment—a far cry from the mainly volunteer groups that traditionally do advocacy work. Consequently, these groups have made some of the most striking advances in the local policy arena. Their work on reducing access to tobacco, for example, has shifted the public debate on tobacco so dramatically that the very future of the tobacco industry is in doubt. This was considered an impossible feat even ten years ago.

This book is written primarily as a resource for these coalitions, especially those just starting out. However, those who are not public health advocates but are interested in developing local policy initiatives will find useful information as well.

The first chapter outlines some of the tensions between program-focused work and engaging in policy development and offers reasons for advocates to undertake local policy work. The next two chapters provide case studies on local policy initiatives from a variety of disciplines—including some outside of traditional public health work. Chapter 4 examines common lessons and provides some "how to" information on the process of developing a policy initiative, from concept to enforcement. Chapter 5 looks specifically at the role of media and offers practical advice for mounting effective media advocacy initiatives. The final chapter explores future trends and challenges to local policy development.

1

TIME TO SHARE THE BURDEN:

Toward Institution-Focused Intervention

> All persons are equally responsible for sharing the burdens—as well
> as the benefits—of protection against death and disability, except
> where unequal burdens result in greater protection for every person,
> especially potential victims of death and disability. In practice this
> means that policies to control the hazards of a given substance,
> service or commodity fall unequally (but still fairly) on those involved
> in the production, provision or consumption of the service,
> commodity or substance.
>
> —DANIEL BEAUCHAMP, PUBLIC HEALTH SCHOLAR [1]

Who are you holding responsible for social problems in this country? A strange question perhaps, but each time we choose an action to address a problem, we also assign responsibility to some group for solving that problem. For example, if you think the answer to the drug problem is reaching young people, then you are placing the responsibility for drug use on their shoulders. Youth violence? Focusing on gun policy or movie violence puts the onus on one set of players and institutions, advocating for mentoring or "scared straight" programs targets another.

Most public health work focuses on individuals as the target for change in addressing social problems. Of course, work with individuals is extremely important and valuable, but institutions—primarily government and corporations—have the greatest impact on social problems. There are good reasons for the emphasis on individuals. Institutional change—and advocacy that targets institutions—is difficult to achieve and risky to attempt because it must challenge business-as-usual in the U.S.

This country has, at the core of its governing philosophy, two principles: the sanctity of the individual and individual rights, and the sanctity of corporate or "free" enterprise. At the core of this philosophy is the belief in the interdependency of "corporate health" and the nation's economic health, as in the old slogan, "What's good for General Motors is good for the country." This sanctity of enterprise, or, actually, the right to profit from enterprise, dictates that corporate regulation, taxation or any policy that places "burdens" on enterprise must be kept to a minimum.

In asserting government's "obligation" to essentially (burden-)free enterprise, corporate interests advocate for policies that place more burdens on the individual. This focus on changing individual behavior and defining public health problems from an individual perspective shifts blame and accountability away from corporate action (or inaction). Yet, corporate activity and government deregulation have had enormous impacts on the public's health.

For example, the siting of toxic waste dumps, regulation of food safety and the availability of healthy food, access to and availability of recreational areas, and adequate income are all important factors in public health. Every one of these factors is largely controlled by corporate action, government action or both. Food safety standards have consistently dropped as the federal government has cut back inspections and safeguards. Where and how jobs are made available and for what wages are all part of a complex interaction between corporate behavior (i.e. where they choose to operate, what wages they offer, etc.) and government regulation (setting minimum or living wage, occupational safety policies, transportation access, etc.).

Poverty, the most significant risk factor for illness and mortality, can be directly linked with high unemployment and lower wages. Poverty rates for families with children headed by persons younger than 30 nearly doubled from 1973 to 1990. The most significant increases in poverty rates during that time were for married couples of all races, with an increase of more than 148 percent. The rate for whites increased 124 percent, for African Americans and Latinos it increased about 45 percent.

While poverty rates rise, wages fall. In 1967, the minimum wage for a full-time employee was enough to keep a family of three above poverty. Today, the minimum wage cannot keep a full-time worker in a family of two above the official poverty line. This is important because most minimum-wage earners are adults, not teens. A third of minimum-wage earners are the sole wage earner in their family.

Higher wage earners are also feeling the pinch. Real wages for college-educated workers dropped 7.5 percent from 1973–1993, while costs for mortgages and most goods and services increased for every worker nationwide. And the future looks dim: wages are expected to drop even more as half of the new jobs created by 2005 will be low-wage jobs requiring no more than a high school education. A 1992 Labor Department study predicts that 30 percent of college graduates between now and 2005 will either face joblessness or underemployment.[2]

Many of the new jobs being created now are temporary, part-time jobs, most of which are without benefits. The number of part-time workers who would rather work full time (known as "involuntary part-time workers") tripled between 1970 and 1993. Economists are predicting that these part-time or "contingent" workers will outnumber full-time permanent employees by the year 2000. Perhaps most telling is that the nation's number-one private employer is Manpower Inc., an agency that places temporary workers. As more workers are forced into part-time, temporary jobs, there will be more families without adequate income, health benefits and access to preventive health care.[3]

Virtually every family has given up the dream of "doing better" than their parents did—except, perhaps, families that include the head of a major corporation. While real wages for most workers trailed behind consumer prices during the 1970s and 1980s, earnings for the average American CEO increased by 514 percent from 1980 through 1993. Corporate profits increased by only 166 percent during the same years.[4]

Corporations now also enjoy more public subsidies than ever before. Companies receive billions of dollars in government grants for everything from research and development to marketing tobacco and alcohol overseas. They also receive billions more in indirect subsidies through tax breaks and incentives. In fact, if companies paid income tax today at the same rate as required by law in 1967, there would be no federal debt. Now, thanks to deregulation and other changes in the tax and regulatory framework, corporate tax rates are about two-thirds lower than they were 30 years ago.

The rationale for this government largesse has been that, in exchange for decreased tax and regulatory burdens, corporations would provide more jobs and thereby greater economic and social stability. They have done neither. From 1980 through 1993, Fortune 500 industrial firms cut nearly 4.4 million jobs. That was one out of four jobs they previously provided. During the same period, sales increased by 1.4 times and assets by 2.3 times, greatly increasing their profits.[5]

The much-touted growth in jobs over roughly the same period has been largely in low-wage and contingent work. From 1979 to 1983, more than three-quarters of net new job growth were low-wage jobs in retail and health care services.[6]

In addition to not providing adequate employment—the backbone of a healthy society—there are those corporations whose very products contribute to undermining the public's health. Tobacco, alcohol, pesticides and herbicides, toxic industrial wastes, and ozone-depleting substances—to name a few—all exact costs upon society. For example, for every retail dollar spent on alcoholic beverages, approximately one dollar of social costs is created. For tobacco, that cost is estimated at three dollars in social costs for every dollar spent on tobacco.[7]

The drain on society from these companies is tremendous. Families can no longer afford to subsidize these companies and fund government programs to address the myriad social costs created by them. Given corporate resources, responsibility, and social and political agency relative to those of individuals, policies that focus on individual behavior alone cannot bring about the fundamental changes required to address the prevention of disease and disability.

Currently, individuals are shouldering much more than their fair share of the responsibility. It's time to develop a new regulatory framework that restores accountability and balance. Such a framework would make much more of an impact than any individual intervention could possibly achieve—even on individual behavior. For example, work in tobacco control has shown us that dramatic reductions in the number of people who smoke can occur when attention is also paid to corporate accountability issues such as industry marketing practices and how and where tobacco is available.

PRODUCTS AND PAYCHECKS: THE NEW ADDICTIONS

We have now entered times in which there is agreement that the four major determinants of physical well being are individual behavior (smoking, lack of exercise), social organization (stress, burn-out), the

physical environment (pollution, workplace) and economic status
(poverty, over-consumption)....Different tools, different actors, different interests are required to affect these health determinants.

—JOHN MCKNIGHT, SOCIOLOGIST AND PIONEER OF ASSET-BASED DEVELOPMENT [8]

Sell them their dreams. Sell them what they longed for and hoped for
and almost despaired of having. Sell them hats by splashing sunlight
across them. Sell them dreams—dreams of country clubs and proms
and visions of what might happen if only. After all, people don't buy
things to have things. They buy things to work for them. They buy
hope—hope for what your merchandise will do for them. Sell them
this hope and you don't have to worry about selling them goods.

—ANNOUNCEMENT AT A 1923 CONVENTION OF DISPLAY MEN [9]

Regulating corporations is difficult not only because of their political power, but also because of their centrality to the nation's economy.
Their rise is a relatively new phenomenon. Less than a century ago, most
of the people in this country were thrifty entrepreneurs who bought
almost everything they owned with cash. Diets were simpler and low on
processed foods. Smoking, and the use of alcohol and other drugs were
less prevalent—especially among young people. Then, something happened that, more than any other factor, transformed Americans'
appetites, habits and quality of life: the rise of the consumer industry.

Before 1880, most people lived and worked on farms. Most businesses (including factories) had fewer than ten workers and were
owned and managed by individuals.[10] Goods and services were produced and distributed locally and regionally for the most part with little
or no marketing to encourage their consumption.

With the advent of consumer corporations came a whole new
economy, one that required the consolidation of markets and the creation of consumer desire and dependence, so that these institutions
could literally bank on large-scale, massive consumption and increasing
profits. By the 1920s, whole new disciplines were created to support
these macroeconomic shifts: investment banking, advertising (a hybrid
of art, aesthetics and industry), fashion modeling and more. At the federal level, the Department of Commerce was created for the purpose of
expanding the corporate form.[11] As William Leach writes in his seminal

book, *Land of Desire: Merchants, Power and the Rise of a New American Culture:*

> The new consumer direction of American culture was also the consequence of alliances among diverse institutions, non-economic and economic, working together in an interlocking circuit of relationships to reinforce the democratization of desire and the cult of the new. National corporations, department stores, investment banks, hotel chains, and the entertainment industry joined this circuit, but so did the Metropolitan Museum of Art and the Brooklyn Museum, the Harvard Business School and the Wharton School....American religious institutions, and the spiritual culture transmitted by them, were transformed by the new mass economy and culture and aided in their creation.[12]

By 1930, the economy of America had been completely transformed. More people depended on corporations for their livelihood. Fewer people worked for themselves. And thanks to the extension of credit and relentless, sophisticated advertising, Americans were consuming goods and services like never before—even if they couldn't really afford them.

The Great Depression, ignited by the stock market crash of October, 1929, was the first, most memorable crisis in the new consumer economy. It was the first time most Americans did not have their own land, their own source of food or some means of livelihood in their control when times got hard. Since then, the underclass of unemployed, landless people has become a fixture in our society, one part of the many tradeoffs inherent in the "consumerization" of American culture.

The Depression demonstrated America's deep dependence on corporations for jobs. The economy had become one circular trail of dominoes, with large corporations at the beginning. These companies had displaced most of the regional and local industry, making the country virtually one market, so that the jobs and livelihood of society in large part depended upon these institutions. In turn, the ability of these corporations to survive and thrive depended on increasing consumer spending, which depended on consumers being employed, and so on.

Corporations quickly exploited this dependence and, by the end of World War II, were collaborating with a vast network of universities, businesses and policy organizations to justify consumerism as the highest evolution of socio-economic organization. It was in this context that the production, marketing and sales of products that had little real value (and some with clearly negative effects) began. Some of the most deleterious products—unsafe toys and textiles for children, or foods lacking nutritional value—appeared in the marketplace justified only by their potential to make a profit. When consumers protested, corporations held the prospect of jobs and consumer choice to the nation's collective head like a gun.

By the 1950s, overconsumption had become patriotic. Newspapers would often scold readers if Christmas sales were too low or if people weren't buying more than they did the year before. It became standard practice for people to identify themselves as consumers as an indication of their stake and commitment as a patriot, as in the common expression, "I'm a taxpayer and a consumer." As a result, government did little to thwart the marketing and consumption of unhealthy products—or promote the consumption of less profitable, healthy ones. Even now, government often operates to the contrary, providing subsidies and tax deductions for marketing and promotions—even for products, like guns, alcohol and tobacco, whose use it is also trying to reduce through tax-supported campaigns. Companies are, for the most part, absolved of any responsibility in creating this culture of desire.

CHOICE VS. THE MARKET

High-fat diets, tobacco use and alcohol consumption create enormous social costs, which are mostly borne by individuals and are usually blamed on personal choices. These choices are in large measure shaped by marketing to consumers. Much of the work of public health is to counter this tremendous desire-creating apparatus, either with relatively meager messages urging discipline or deprivation, or with programmatic efforts to influence people through public education, mentoring programs and the like.

Moving beyond these approaches to address the media onslaught that feeds unhealthy behaviors has been difficult, as corporate interests dominate public discourse on the impact of advertising. Thanks to corporate disinformation, it is conventional wisdom among lay people and the academy that the billions of dollars these companies spend on advertising has no effect on individual choices. One moment's reflection away from this propaganda would strongly suggest otherwise. The alcohol industry spends $1.09 billion a year, or more than $124,000 per hour, on advertising.[13] Much of this advertising is in media whose major audience is youth. Although the alcohol industry claims that the purpose of advertising is to increase market share, not recruit new drinkers, studies by Wallack, Cassady and Grube suggest otherwise. Young people exposed to alcohol advertising are more likely to think positively about alcohol consumption and indicate a desire to drink in the future.[14]

Clearly, the marketing and creation of desire for products that undermine our health has had a major effect on our society. It will take more than a good counter-advertising campaign to un-sell a century of marketing so sophisticated and so far-reaching that it has virtually rewoven our social fabric.

Today, the greatest barrier to healthy, people-centered policies is opposition by business. Right or wrong, efforts to regulate advertising, reduce product availability or address corporate tax policy are met with company threats of massive unemployment and economic destabilization. We talk health, they talk jobs. Even with all the evidence on the health dangers of tobacco consumption, at the time of this writing, federal regulation of the industry proceeds at a slow pace due mostly to fears of massive job and economic losses.

In many ways, the public's health and safety are placed on one side of the scale and economic development on the other. It is health or jobs; regulation or jobs. As a society we must ask ourselves: How much is a job worth? An annual death toll of 400,000 people as a result of tobacco use? The extinction of 1,000 species due to land development and industrial pollution? How much is consumer choice worth? The relentless laboring of young girls in crowded, dim factories to make more products more cheaply? The generation of more pollution that creates an ever bigger hole in the ozone layer? The real public health challenge of the twenty-first century is how we imagine a new set of economic relationships, one that doesn't require so much harm in the balance.

Perhaps the most pervasive public health problem we face is *our society's addiction to the profits* that come from creating addiction. It is this money that ties us to the very *structure* that requires problems, like tobacco and alcohol addiction, in order to thrive. We are told we cannot implement effective public health strategies, such as increasing taxes on unhealthy products or restricting their advertising, because of the impact these actions would have on profits. Clearly, saving the profits is considered more important than saving our people. Until we address this fundamental contradiction we can never truly heal anyone. We will simply continue to bandage the wounded and teach the able-bodied to duck.

BOOTS VS. NECK MUSCLES: BEYOND PEOPLE AS PROBLEMS

How does it feel to be a problem?

—W.E.B. DUBOIS[15]

For many of us working in public health, programs are the key to making change because we think of our work as "fixing" people with problems. We organize our work according to the limb, organ, or addiction our funding requires us to target and we design programs to reach the "problem people." Programs are designed, in the main, to provide *information* so that individuals "at risk" can "know better," which in turn will cause them to "do better."

This emphasis on educational programs is based on the assumption that the fundamental problem individuals and communities face is lack of information: "They" just don't know any better. Even those who profess to be community organizers lean heavily on information (more commonly called political education) as a motivator for action. Flyers, mass media and teach-ins often form the core of advocacy activities.

Disfranchised communities are bombarded daily with information they can do little with. Colorful ad campaigns and brochures urging residents to eat better and exercise more often appear in neighborhoods where there are neither grocery stores nor places to play. Women are told they must dress differently and modify how and when they travel in order to avoid assault in areas where there is poor land-use planning and inadequate lighting.

The fact is there's only so much that information can do to improve social conditions because, contrary to conventional wisdom, information is not power. Power is having the resources to make changes and choices; to be heard; and to define, control, defend and promote one's interests. Many of the problems facing communities stem from the lack of power—not lack of information. Poverty, exploitation and unequal access to goods and services are all root causes for virtually every social ill in our society. Addressing these problems will require addressing the imbalance of power, or resources, to advance a social change agenda.

It's not that educational programs don't help. They have a purpose and there are certainly important benefits that are derived from these interventions. Raising awareness of certain problems and ways to address them is a useful tool in making change. Organizing and social change strategies and educational programs are all necessary. But there is a difference. It is clear that environmental factors—poverty, sexism, poor quality education, etc.—are stressors that affect an individual's quality of life. They are like a boot on an individual's neck. Of course, people respond differently: some travel very far with these burdens; others are crushed early on. Educational programs are designed to strengthen individuals. They help participants build stronger "neck muscles" so that they can travel longer under life's burdens. Social change strategies, on the other hand, are targeted at the "boot," or burden, to help address some of the environmental barriers.

It has been argued that information is the most important thing one can offer because it motivates people to act. There is some truth to this.

However, it is not information about the problem that catalyzes action but information that also includes doable, realistic ways to address the problem at hand.

In his book, *Domination and the Arts of Resistance: Hidden Transcripts,* James Scott examines more than one thousand years of rebellion among the oppressed. His research asserts the existence of what he calls the "hidden transcript," private discourse of the oppressed that takes place out of the view of the dominant class. This transcript, according to Scott, is comprised of the stories, actions, jokes, fantasies, dreams and plain speaking of the subordinated that are not "safe" to say to the oppressor. Scott writes:

> For most subordinate groups, the social locations in which one can speak with real safety are narrowly restricted. Generally speaking, the smaller and more intimate the group, the safer the possibilities for free expression. The more effective dominant groups are in preventing subordinates from assembling in substantial numbers free of surveillance, the smaller the social scope of the hidden transcript. Thus, for example, the effective social reach of the hidden transcript under normal circumstances might not extend much beyond, say, one plantation, one hamlet of untouchables, the neighborhood pub, or perhaps merely the family.[16]

Rap music is an important example of both the potential within the hidden transcript and the need to link the hidden "conversation" with concrete action and hope for change. Rap music is one of very few venues for expressing rage at the status quo as well as holding a candid discussion of social issues. Of course, much of it is commodified, contradictory and not particularly profound; but most of it chronicles the lived experience of a significant number of young people in America.

With the national distribution of what some call "reality rap," previously isolated groups (mostly African-American and Latino males) now have a sense of community, that there are lots of people like them going through the same despair and facing the same tough decisions. This sense of validation has endowed rap music with a power rarely observed in popular music. However, without links to concrete action for change, it is just music for nodding heads and commiserating.

In barber shops, at kitchen tables and encoded in popular youth culture, the hidden transcript unfolds. Although people are not talking about data and theory in the supermarket line, they often already possess an awareness and analysis of the social issues that affect their lives. For example, it's not that disfranchised communities don't know about police brutality or poor quality schools, or that these are serious problems. In fact, there is plenty of evidence to suggest that these are common topics in the conversation taking place away from the surveillance of those "outside" of these communities. One need only to listen to rap or country music or read opinion polls to see evidence of public awareness of a wide range of issues.

Therefore, it is not giving people information that's key to motivating them to act, but validating their perceptions *and conveying a sense that the change they dare to imagine in these private spaces is achievable and desired by a great many others.*

This validation occurs when an individual or group "breaks out" and publicly articulates the hidden transcript. This moment of unveiling is key as it provides previously isolated groups a context and sense that their beliefs are shared by the majority. As Scott writes, "The process, then, is more one of recognizing close relatives of one's hidden transcript rather than of filling essentially empty heads with novel ideas."[17]

The Million Man March is a great example of validation of the hidden transcript. The public call for a gathering of a million African-American men in the nation's capital touched a nerve in African-American communities. The "hidden conversation" about alienation and racism was unveiled. Millions of people responded to hearing "their issues" articulated.

The best work in local policy development gets beyond education and leverages the issues that already concern communities into concrete action. Too often, activists see the work of organizing as "filling essentially empty heads" with our "novel ideas." We must, instead, recognize that there are numerous, atomized conversations going on about social change. Our job is to let people know that they are not isolated in their thinking and, further, there is something concrete that can be done to make things better. In this way, we can make a public counterpoint or "validation" that contradicts the dominant transcript of apathy and complacency. It will require that we keep our ear close to the ground so that we can articulate ideas that resonate (or, as Scott would say, are "close relatives") with the values and dreams folk currently hold.

If utilized, this process can have profound implications for the work of social change. Instead of flyers that are designed to shock or educate, materials would have language that draws on familiar themes in neighborhoods and invite residents to join in something concrete, practical and within their sphere of influence. Activists would spend less time criticizing rap music and instead, listen to the fantasies of power and rebellion, the cries for help there, and recognize opportunities for common ground. Of course, the changes must go beyond *how* we communicate. They must also affect *what* we communicate. In short, it is far more important to communicate that something can be done than it is to communicate what's going wrong.

Local policy initiatives offer an effective way to engage communities in realistic action. When done effectively, campaigns are developed to address issues of concern to communities; activists articulate those issues in common, everyday language, and work collaboratively with residents to develop practical, easy-to-understand initiatives.

The case studies in the next two chapters are good examples of these kinds of policy initiatives. In each case, community organizing was central—more central than the passage of the ordinance itself. For the efforts featured in these chapters, building a power base and addressing the real needs of the communities were paramount; the ordinance was simply a means to an end. Advocates can take a cue from these exemplary efforts and build a varied toolbox of action for community change, of which policymaking is only a part.

2

AN AGENDA OF SUBSTANCE:

Grassroots Efforts to Reduce Alcohol and Tobacco Problems

Mr. Coke said to Mr. Mayor
you know we gotta process like Ice T's hair
We put up the funds for your re-election campaign
Oh, uh, waiter, bring some more champagne…
Don't worry 'bout the Urban League or Jesse Jackson
My man down at Marlboro donated a fat sum…

—"BIG CATS, BIGGA FISH," THE COUP, (HIP-HOP ARTISTS)[1]

I'm saying the [St. Ides malt liquor] potency is high, and it's targeted at youth. Anything is permissible as long as it's for dollars. The advertising, it's tied to gangs and sexual promiscuity. If gangs and promiscuity are not major agendas that have to be addressed in the African-American community, there are none. They are talking dollars. We are talking lives.

—PAUL KELLY, LATE ACTIVIST WITH CHICAGO'S CITYWIDE COALITION AGAINST TOBACCO AND ALCOHOL BILLBOARDS [2]

It's long been known that poverty and racism are significant risk factors for injury, death and disease.[3] It is important to note, however, that the link between alcohol problems and poverty exists not because those in low-income communities drink more. In fact, they drink less. Rather, the conditions of poverty create an environment that increases the risk of alcohol problems when drinking does occur (i.e., lack of access to medical care, high crime, unsafe neighborhoods). That's why, for a growing number of organizations, reducing the availability of alcohol has been a key strategy in addressing both community development and health status.[4]

Numerous studies have shown that there are more places to buy alcohol in poor communities of color than in other communities. As a neighborhood declines, the number of alcohol outlets increases, replacing other local businesses, further undermining the local economy and serving as a destabilizing force. The nexus is clear: strategies that address economic underdevelopment and joblessness in poor, inner-city communities help reduce risk to public health and safety from alcohol-related behaviors.[5]

Over the past 30 years, community groups in poor neighborhoods have organized around the easy availability of alcohol as a way to reduce risk in their communities. They observed that urban communities of color were targeted with certain alcohol products that were not made available or even advertised in white neighborhoods. Fortified wines and beers (malt liquors) were featured in culturally specific advertising and these ads often promoted the very behaviors (i.e., public drinking, violence, over-consumption, etc.) that community groups were seeking to eliminate. In the late 1980s, tobacco became more of an issue as ads targeted the most potent and deadly (high tar, mentholated) cigarettes to these communities.[6]

Residents also felt that the advertising was offensive. Olde English 800 billboards, for example, promoted the product's strength, by indirectly comparing the beer to cocaine (calling the brew "eight ball," a slang term for the drug) and featured scantily clad women. One Seagrams billboard featured an African-American couple in an intimate pose: a man with his face in a woman's open blouse. This angered residents who felt these companies were operating from a cynical view of their communities as places where anything goes.

Discriminatory patterns in local zoning law left residents with few options for regulatory relief. Inner-city communities, regardless of how residential they were, were zoned for business use, which meant large numbers of billboards, excessive ad signage on retail outlets and too many stores selling alcohol in these neighborhoods were all permissible. Some residents endured billboards on their homes or in their yards that were permitted by landlords and sanctioned by local planning authorities. This local experience of alcohol and tobacco as blight literally shoved targeted marketing and product availability in the face of urban communities.[7]

The following stories describe how two inner-city coalitions, on opposite sides of the country, leveraged grassroots organizing and policy savvy to reduce the availability of alcohol and the prevalence of alcohol advertising in their communities.

Getting L.A. Development Off the Bottle: The Community Coalition for Substance Abuse Prevention and Treatment

The Community Coalition for Substance Abuse Prevention and Treatment (CCSAPT) was founded in 1990 by a diverse group of activists, service providers and people in recovery with funding from the federal Center for Substance Abuse Prevention. From the beginning, CCSAPT employed grassroots advocacy and policy change as primary tools to address alcohol and other drug problems in South Central Los Angeles.

"We wanted to address the drug epidemic in South L.A. Our first thought was that it was rooted in the economic and social divestment in the area," says CCSAPT's assistant director, Sylvia Castillo. "We thought that the reason individuals were using drugs was to medicate the pain of racism and unemployment. So, built on that, what do you do to respond? One of the ways we felt we needed to respond—and respond immediately—was to organize individuals to see the power that they had. We felt there was a need to involve people in leadership development to take positions, to have a say in what was happening not only at the neighborhood level but at the city level, at the level of policymaking."[8]

More often than not, South Central is portrayed in the media as a set of mean streets full of violence and abject poverty with little opportunity for those who reside there. In reality, the 40-square-mile area where CCSAPT works is more complex than that. It is one of the most ethnically diverse communities in the United States. About a third of its residents do live in poverty, and the median income in the area is only slightly more than half of the median income for Los Angeles as a whole. But despite areas of high crime, there are many older, stable neighborhoods whose residents have lived in the area for decades.

Like many inner-city communities, South Central L.A. has gone through many changes. Half a century ago, people came from Texas, Louisiana, Arkansas and other parts of the South to settle in the area for the many manufacturing jobs nearby. The plentiful job market allowed residents to enjoy a level prosperity impossible back home. They bought homes and rental property, built churches and social clubs and opened small businesses that catered to the growing community of Southerners.

As the community increasingly became home to African Americans, white-owned banks and other businesses reduced their investments there. Some manufacturing firms moved out of the area, while others fell prey to the larger macroeconomic shifts, such as changes in production and materials and consumer preferences that affected the manufacturing sector nationwide. As businesses left or folded, unemployment and poverty spiraled upward.

Much of the retail sector was abandoning South Central as well. In their place came smaller, family-owned and run (or "mom and pop") stores, that provided a small selection of food, groceries and other convenience items. Prior to 1965, California grocery stores were subject to price controls that maintained uniform pricing for many grocery items regardless of store size or sales volume. While these laws were in effect, mom and pop stores and big grocery chains had much the same prices. With the repeal of these laws (ostensibly to spur greater competition), smaller stores suddenly found themselves greatly "out discounted" by larger chains. Store deregulation also lifted caps on food pricing, allowing smaller stores to raise prices greatly, and decreased the number of site inspections. The result was often high-priced, poor-quality food at fewer retail outlets in inner-city communities. Those residents who could shopped at larger supermarkets further away, making the neighborhood stores more and more dependent on non-perishable (and more profitable) items—like alcohol and tobacco. By 1970, there were more liquor stores than any other business in South Central.[9]

The South Central Organizing Committee (SCOC), a coalition of 22 churches, organized around problem alcohol outlets in 1983. SCOC's work focused, at first, on increasing law enforcement activity in and around the stores. In an eight-week period, more than 600 alcohol-related arrests were made. However, the police department claimed it could not continue to make monitoring these outlets a priority, citing mounting crime and budgetary constraints. SCOC turned from law enforcement to the less labor-intensive approaches of land-use and planning regulation.

Their efforts culminated in a city ordinance in 1984 that placed conditions on new alcohol outlets in an identified problem area.

Although the ordinance did a good job of regulating new outlets, it was virtually powerless over existing ones that were "grandfathered in" as "deemed approved" without any additional conditions from the city.[10] After that victory, SCOC moved on to other issues.

By 1992, a study by the University of Southern California School of Medicine showed most South Central census tracts had more than twice the number of alcohol outlets prescribed by California law (one outlet per 2,500 persons) and that there was a positive correlation between the high density of alcohol outlets and an increase in violent crime in the area. In fact, the USC study showed that in a Los Angeles County community with 50,000 residents and 100 existing outlets, 10 more places selling alcohol would produce 25 additional violent crimes annually.[11] In 1992, South Central had 728 alcohol outlets; this number was more than the *statewide* number of alcohol outlets in 11 states.

By the time CCSAPT emerged in 1990, abandonment of the community by business and government had created high rates of unemployment and poverty as well as an overconcentration of liquor stores. It was CCSAPT's belief that the prevalence of liquor stores was "cannibalizing" other businesses. While other retail establishments did not want to locate in areas with a high density of liquor stores, these stores were increasing to profit off of what residents referred to as "the misery market" of poor, unemployed drinkers, some of them underage.

High numbers of unemployed people loitering near stores (as well as criminal activity like drug dealing and solicitation by some unscrupulous owners) made the outlets magnets for crime. Further, alcohol products targeted to inner-city communities, most notably the introduction of more potent malt liquor in much larger bottles, were transforming drinking patterns: more drinkers were drinking larger amounts than ever before. This meant there were more intoxicated people with compromised judgment, putting both drinkers and passersby at greater risk of injury and violent crime.

In addition, the demographics of store owners were changing. Increasingly, immigrants new to the community and culture were investing in these stores because they had few opportunities for entrepreneurship elsewhere. The Small Business Administration, for example, encouraged loan applicants to open liquor stores because of their profitability.[12] Mounting tensions between storeowners and residents reached fever pitch with the 1991 shooting of African-American teenager Latasha Harlan by a Korean grocer in a dispute over a container of orange juice.

Since its founding, CCSAPT's number-one priority has been to engage as many community residents as possible in grassroots efforts to turn things around. Its goal is to build an institution whose leadership reflects the community. The staff leadership of CCSAPT, though trained medical professionals, are long-time activists and organizers. CCSAPT's executive director, Karen Bass, and assistant director, Sylvia Castillo, shared a history of progressive political activism in a wide range of arenas. They adeptly combined their background in health care with their organizing experience to conceptualize and lead what is essentially a social justice approach to alcohol and other drug problems.

The Coalition wanted to get beyond the repressive criminal justice orientation that characterized the government's "war on drugs" and address root causes. South Los Angeles, like most inner-city communities, was under siege by law enforcement. Indiscriminate police sweeps that arrested large numbers of neighborhood youth, and aggressive "criminal loitering" laws made the area feel more like a militarized zone than a set of neighborhoods. According to Castillo:

> We wanted to have a progressive response to what was, at that point, repressive policies like [so called] gang sweeps, Operation Cul de Sac, Operation Battering Ram and [federal "drug czar"] William Bennett's War on Drugs. The only way to have an effective response was to organize the masses.[13]

The Coalition started with door-to-door surveys of 1,100 residents in South Central Los Angeles neighborhoods. Not surprisingly, after nearly 20 years of controversy and advocacy around alcohol outlets predating CCSAPT, the survey revealed a strong sentiment against the overconcentration of alcohol outlets and related problems. The Coalition leveraged the survey into an organizing opportunity by identifying not only the issues but also the people who would commit to working on them. As Karen Bass recalls:

> We chose to do the needs assessment in a way that could train ourselves and our membership in community-organizing techniques. When we started the partnership we wanted to figure out how to work on a drug and alcohol issue and organize a neighborhood to fight for change....To me, the liquor store issue proved an opportunity, and I knew there was a history of organizing on that issue. The survey verified that the issue was still viable, and in August of 1991 we made an organizational decision to take it on.[14]

Once the decision was made, the Coalition worked with the local office of the state Alcoholic Beverage Control Department and the Los Angeles Police Department to identify the extent of the problem. Organizing residents to help gather information, the group mapped the number of outlets, licensees and the location of and incidents around problem outlets. They also mapped what other businesses existed in the area, which highlighted the overconcentration of alcohol outlets and the lack of other business establishments.

These organizing efforts, central to CCSAPT's work, continued as residents participated in presenting the information to public officials and the Coalition pressed the city into action.

In early 1992 the city proposed to eliminate public review of alcohol licenses for grocery stores and businesses with 1,400 or more square feet. This move was designed to circumvent expected public opposition to an alcohol outlet as part of a new market in the South Central neighborhood. Touting the proposal as an economic development plan, Mayor Tom Bradley claimed it would remove "red tape" to make way for greater business investment in the area. The market owners promoted the business as a much-needed provider of food and other goods in the underdeveloped neighborhood. But the Coalition was clear that the store in question was, in the main, another alcohol outlet. Sylvia Castillo commented on the mayor's proposal: "It was going to take away from residents the due process right to decide whether or not a particular grocery store should have a liquor license."[15]

Because of its organizing work on the mapping project, CCSAPT was in a strong position to respond. In February 1992, the Coalition staged a protest in front of Los Angeles City Hall in order to push the mayor and city council on the issue. Thanks to this community pressure, the city was forced to withdraw the proposal. The Coalition had helped officials see the connection between outlet overconcentration and economic disinvestment. As a result, the city established the Mayor's Task Force on Problem Liquor Stores.

CCSAPT organized more than 100 people to come out for the first task force meeting. Residents took advantage of the opportunity to air their concerns to the mayor, planning commissioner and zoning administrator. The residents gave testimony on the crime, neglect, illegal activities and other problems in and around their neighborhood liquor stores. Residents were also able to find how little the city had done to address these issues.

Says Sylvia Castillo:

> [We discovered that there had been] no revocation of licenses
> of problem liquor stores....We were really frustrated that the
> city had never identified what could be the processes that they
> could use in order to hold these merchants accountable to elim-
> inate the public nuisances. Ironically, this meeting was the day
> before our city went up in flames.[16]

THE CIVIL UNREST

On April 29, 1992, South Central Los Angeles was "ground zero"
in a multi-cultural, multi-city rebellion that was sparked by the acquittal of three white police officers charged with the beating of an African
American named Rodney King. Police brutality in African-American
communities is by no means new. What made the King beating different was that it was captured on videotape by a white photographer who
released the tape to news outlets nationwide. The brutal savagery captured on tape angered many, but the acquittal of the police officers
involved in the face of such evidence pushed some to the boiling point.
The acquittal, many felt, was part of a long history of bias, neglect and
disfranchisement; they were not going to take it any more.

Among those arrested during the Los Angeles unrest, 45 percent
were Latino, 41 percent African American and 12 percent were white.
Sixty percent had no criminal record prior to their arrest. Fifty-eight
people were killed over the three days, 44 of whom were African
American or Latino.[17] More than half of South Central's 728 alcohol
outlets were damaged during the three-day insurgence. About 200 of
them were completely destroyed.[18] Alcohol outlets were far and away
the most likely target for destruction, followed by check-cashing
places.[19] The damage provided more evidence of how deeply residents
resented the blight and other problems associated with overconcentration of liquor stores.

The Coalition immediately understood that, although tragic in
many ways, the civil unrest created opportunities to galvanize what was
clearly strong community sentiment around issues of economic disinvestment and public safety related to outlet overconcentration. Meanwhile, city government was working feverishly to get the businesses
that were damaged or destroyed on the fast track toward rebuilding. To
facilitate the process, a newly hired city planning director drafted the
Emergency Rebuild L.A. Ordinance, which proposed to eliminate com-

munity input on rebuilding by businesses affected by the civil unrest.

City officials were completely unprepared for the community outrage that followed their announcement of the proposed ordinance. Residents flooded city phone lines urging that liquor stores not be rebuilt. With the stores gone, according to callers, neighborhoods had become much calmer and quieter—the first such lull in crime, said residents, in many years.[20]

In response to pressure by CCSAPT to get alcohol outlets off the fast track, the city established the Mayor's South Central Community/ Merchant Liquor Task Force as an early concession. But the task force did not address the rebuild ordinance; it was merely to provide a venue for dialogue between merchants, city officials and community leaders. The city was clear: alcohol outlets needed to stay on the rebuild fast track.

Fortunately, two key officials were opposed to the rebuild ordinance: city council members Mark Ridley-Thomas and Rita Walters. Both their districts were in south Los Angeles and both had a history of community activism in the area. Ridley-Thomas and Walters were strong allies of the Coalition and had worked with CCSAPT on many occasions. Prior to their tenure on the city council, both had been active in SCOC's earlier efforts to regulate alcohol outlets.

Council member Walters proposed amendments to the draft rebuild ordinance that exempted alcohol outlets, pawn shops, swap meets, gun shops and auto-wrecking shops from the fast-track provisions. For more than two weeks, the Coalition mobilized support for the amendments that resulted in hundreds of calls to council members, packed council meetings and media attention. The hard work paid off. The amendments were enacted when the ordinance passed in mid-May.

With alcohol outlets exempted from fast-track approval, the Coalition moved into the next phase of its campaign: organizing community action to keep problem outlets from rebuilding. On June 1, at a meeting CCSAPT organized, about 200 people called for a moratorium on the rebuilding of alcohol outlets. They decided to circulate a petition showing support for the moratorium, with a goal of collecting 1,000 signatures. Using volunteers and four staff hired as the "street action team," CCSAPT gathered more than 7,500 signatures in just ten days. They revised the goal upward to 20,000. On August 1, the Coalition delivered 35,000 signatures to the mayor.[21]

The Coalition had mobilized a formidable group of residents, organizations and institutions to collect the signatures. The faith community was particularly important to their organizing efforts, as CCSAPT effectively tapped into South Central's long history of faith-based activism. Groups like SCOC, the movement to provide sanctuary to Central American political refugees, and the local chapter of the Southern Christian Leadership Conference (the ecumenical political organization founded by Dr. Martin Luther King, Jr.), had long engaged their membership in the political issues of the day. They joined the Campaign to Rebuild L.A. without Liquor Stores with enthusiasm, providing volunteers and meeting spaces, among other resources.

In addition to organizing community support for the rebuild moratorium, the Coalition also developed a plan to support outlet owners who wished to convert their businesses to less harmful uses. Council members Mike Woo and Ridley-Thomas worked with CCSAPT and willing outlet operators to provide incentives for conversion, such as tax credits and low-interest loans. A study conducted at the request of the city council found that Laundromats and food outlets, among other services, were in great need in the area. CCSAPT lobbied the city council for support for owners who wished to open up new businesses that met residents' needs. Recalls Castillo:

> That meant us working cooperatively with the Korean merchants who wanted to stay in the community and were looking for resources to stay and do some other kind of business. We were doing concrete acts of solidarity that were going to bring a change to the merchants' ability to rebuild. And we were also hosting meetings with those merchants and community members to think through if they were going to rebuild and if there is something they wanted to do to elicit the goodwill of the community, there's this opportunity for a new social contract. Let's walk through what the Laundromat should look like, what should be the standards of operations, how can the community be vigilant so it won't deteriorate.[22]

COLOR ADJUSTMENT:
DEALING WITH MEDIA'S NARROW VIEW

You would never know of CCSAPT's efforts to reach out to merchants from the news. Generally, news media took great pains to portray the unrest and its aftermath as either a black-white or, later, a black-Korean conflict. The partnership between council members Woo (a Chinese American) and Ridley-Thomas (an African American) was downplayed in virtually all news coverage. When it came to the Coalition, the press was only interested in black spokespersons, faces that could illustrate the story much of the press had already chosen to portray.

Sylvia Castillo, herself a Latina, led the campaign and was its first organizer. She was supported by a multi-ethnic street action team and by volunteers who were residents of the black and brown communities where the Coalition organized. Through careful attention to diversity in their recruitment efforts, CCSAPT built a coalition that was truly representative of South Los Angeles—a fact that stumped a press used to seeing urban issues in black and white. Castillo recalls one typical interaction in which media ignored the Latino component of CCSAPT's work:

> There was a national magazine that covered the process we were taking people through to prepare them for the rebuild hearings. They had cameras and they would only focus the cameras on the African-American side of the church. On the Latino side of the church, where the translation was going on, there were no cameras....When we saw the piece we called them up and we wrote a letter and we essentially said, "What kind of story was that? That's not what you came to see." The editor basically said it was too difficult for people in the Midwest to understand black-brown [unity]. The equation for them was black [versus] Korean.[23]

The Coalition didn't sit by and let themselves be victimized by the press. They made sure to let the media know of inaccuracies right away. As Castillo recalls:

> We always responded. If there was bad press, we would call them. We'd say, "Come down here. You wrote in an article that it was thus and so and that's the incorrect equation. We ask you to come here to our meetings. We ask you to go door-to-door with us. We ask you to come to the hearings. We want you to come to the hearings when it's an African-American store owner." It was holding the press accountable and it was also doing our own press—in op-ed pieces. We would do press events where we would create a message that said, "This is about public safety." We said to the press, "We're gonna check you when you do this [inaccurate reporting]. We're gonna check you with other press. And no, we're not going to give you any more interviews." [24]

BUILDING RELATIONSHIPS THROUGH WORK

The 1992 civil unrest exposed a raw nerve in Los Angeles. Television news stories relayed pictures to the nation of a deeply divided city. Activists who prided themselves on what they thought were successful multi-racial coalitions and alliances were shocked at how fragile long-standing relationships had become in the wake of the rebellion. Emotions ran deep and old allies had to work hard to maintain and repair relationships that wore under the stress of competing concerns. There were Asian-American activists who were working to heal increasingly anti-immigrant sentiment made worse by the unrest. African-American activists felt slighted and even oppressed by merchants and wanted redress.

CCSAPT was committed to building a permanent coalition that reflected the primarily Latino and African-American communities that made up South Central. Recruitment, leadership development and other organizing efforts purposefully focused on building strong relationships across race and ethnicity. The Coalition's approach began with making sure staff and members were clear on the importance of building a democratic, representative organization and were committed to working toward that end. They knew it wouldn't be easy but felt it was important, as an organization comprised of people of color, to take the leadership to work through issues that came up. In this atmosphere, members would take it upon themselves to correct those who made comments or acted in ways that were prejudicial or bigoted. Most often, someone from the same ethnic group would hold the "offender" accountable and set them straight. Says Castillo:

> Having individuals who were Latino and African American with a set of politics and with the capacity to struggle, to engage people in the struggle to move them beyond their own little perception of the power relations—like somehow black folk had more than us or that Latinos were taking away what little black folks had—that seemed to be real important.[25]

The group decided early on that they would not engage in formal mediation and conflict resolution activities, but would build in natural learning opportunities through work. As Castillo says, "The bottom line is that we have to share space." For example, if there were more Spanish-speaking residents at a meeting than not, the meeting was conducted in Spanish and then translated for English speakers. This way, everyone had the experience of depending on a translator in order to participate. It helped to change the power dynamic.

They also did a lot of "fellowship" work. Food at meetings, acknowledging the fruits of their collaboration along the way, and constant leadership development helped to sustain the Coalition for the long and often convoluted process of the rebuild hearings.

KEEPIN' IT REAL IN "LEGAL LAND"

Despite the pressure and the press attention the Coalition brought, the city refused to acquiesce to the Coalition's demands for a moratorium on the rebuilding of alcohol outlets in South Central. The city did require that hearings be held prior to rebuild permits being issued for alcohol outlets. But the hearings would only be to determine conditions to be imposed on the applicants to help prevent "nuisance activities" at the site. The process for shutting down a problem liquor store was made more complex as the city attorney (fearful of being sued by the retailers) tacked on the additional step of a revocation hearing from a separate agency.

To prepare for the rebuild hearings, CCSAPT developed a two-pronged approach. The first was to document any problems that had existed prior to the unrest at or around a liquor store seeking to rebuild. A volunteer group that included researchers and regulatory experts developed easy-to-use documentation forms in English and Spanish; residents could fill them out or have volunteers record the information for them.

Second, the Coalition provided training and support, including role-playing, so that members could participate fully in the rebuild hearings and media coverage about them. In each neighborhood where an alcohol outlet was up for permit, CCSAPT met with local residents to review the documentation of any problems with that site and mobilized them for the hearing. Thus, residents who attended a hearing were there because the issue struck very close to home. This helped them get through the tediousness of the hearing process.

Over an 18-month period, CCSAPT mobilized 1,400 residents to attend hearings involving 59 liquor stores. For many members, it was the first time they went to city hall to have their say. In the end, CCSAPT's organizing helped build a savvy leadership base that was increasingly comfortable with maneuvering the city government system. By 1994, of the almost 250 stores destroyed, only 56 permits had been granted. Of those, only a few stores opted to rebuild. Merchants who were upset by the conditions on their rebuild permits that result-ed from the hearings claimed they were effectively shut down by the provisions.[26]

At the national level, the alcohol industry watched developments in Los Angeles with great concern, as articles in trade publications pre-dicted that Los Angeles' "regulatory fever" would spread nationwide. Already, several California cities were embroiled in pitched battles over additional regulations for alcohol outlets. The industry felt it was time to fight back.

CCSAPT PREPARES TO GO TO COURT

With funding from national alcohol companies, merchants who had owned alcohol outlets in South Central L.A. organized their own petitions, mobilized members to attend hearings, and generated phone calls to elected officials. Their goal was to pressure the city council to eliminate resident input in the hearing process. Despite their efforts, the city did not yield to their demands either. In response, with the help of the Beer Institute and other large alcohol lobbies, the local retailer asso-ciations filed suit against the city.

While the city attorney hoped to avoid legal action through nego-tiation, CCSAPT saw the need to prepare for a lawsuit early on. They began collaborating with the local Legal Aid Foundation to identify legal strategies and to ensure that documentation and testimony at the rebuild hearings were effective and compelling. They developed three primary strategies in a comprehensive approach to reducing outlets: community organizing to keep stores from rebuilding; advocacy for con-version of outlets to other uses; and defending the community's legal rights. The legal battle was a tactic for the Coalition but not its primary effort. As always, organizing was the number one priority. However, the Coalition was committed to dealing with the lawsuit and resulting media coverage as needs arose.

The Coalition weighed its options carefully and decided to seek intervenor status when it felt that the city would probably not defend the hearing process vigorously. As an intervenor, the Coalition could join the lawsuit as an interested party, argue its case against the plain-tiffs and participate in the proceedings through an attorney without being a co-defendant. Intervenor status would also give it a say in any settlement negotiations—which the Coalition wanted to prevent. Legal Aid Foundation attorneys Mary Lee and Bill Lee developed the strategy to file for the intervenor status and conducted the case on behalf of the Coalition. Largely thanks to their efforts, the city's position was affirmed all the way to the Court of Appeals and still stands.

The industry didn't stop at the lawsuit, however. In May, 1993, alcohol lobbyists convinced state Assemblymember Paul Horcher to author Assembly Bill 1974, which, if passed, would override the Los Angeles rebuild policy by guaranteeing all outlets the right to rebuild without going through the process. All the hard work to establish community input in the rebuild process would be wiped out by a single piece of legislation. The bill caught activists by surprise; they were working on their own legislation to help address state preemption (areas of the law where state governance supersedes local authority) so they could expand local authority to regulate alcohol in their communities.

Thanks to a full-time effort by CCSAPT staff and volunteers, AB 1974 was stalled for more than a year. Horcher made one last surprise attempt to resurrect the bill. This, too, was defeated by community pressure augmented with the support of activists statewide.

LOOKING TO THE FUTURE

The Coalition's work yielded important and lasting effects on its community and on its organization. Its careful attention to alliance-building helped to forge strong relationships between African-American and Latino residents, forming the basis for continued work together on a wide range of issues. They built a strong community base and, with it, increased credibility in the community, which expanded their capacity to take up other initiatives. Strong alliances, a large base and a high degree of credibility yielded real dividends in the policy arena as well: policymakers paid attention to the Coalition, making it a bona fide player at city hall and at the state level.

Today, CCSAPT continues to work on alcohol and other drug issues as part of their commitment to community public health and safety. A strong and growing youth component (see Chapter 4) has become increasingly central to its efforts, as the demographics in South Central shift from older homeowners and homemakers to younger (mainly Latina) residents. In planning for the long haul, Castillo articulates the challenge ahead:

> If we are going to do leadership development, [encouraging] community involvement in advocacy, how do we then system-atize it so that long after certain organizers leave we have the

methods in place, we're training people in a set of politics and we institutionalize it so it's a permanent feature of the community?[27]

The answer lies in the Coalition's own methods of continuously refining its practices and taking its lead—and its leadership—from the community.

Grandparents On the March: Baltimore's Citywide Coalition Works to Reduce Alcohol and Tobacco Billboards

Baltimore's Citywide Liquor Coalition for Better Laws and Regulations (CWLC) is a group of primarily older, African-American neighborhood activists working to improve the quality of life in Baltimore's inner city. Made up of more than 100 neighborhood associations, churches and civic groups, CWLC is organized and staffed by the Citizens Planning and Housing Association (CPHA), Baltimore's oldest citizen action organization.

CWLC has been working to address issues of alcohol and tobacco marketing and availability since the late 1980s. Early victories included getting a state law enacted in 1992 that restricted 200 of 600 taverns from selling alcohol for consumption off premises without a package store license.

Although the law was a compromise from the original target of all 600 taverns, it also limited business hours to between 9 a.m. and midnight, and required the taverns to close on Sundays.

In a 1986 campaign, CWLC worked with another local group, the Coalition for Beautiful Neighborhoods, to secure the removal of more than 1,200 illegal "junior" billboards attached to the walls of liquor stores or convenience stores selling alcohol. These signs usually measured five-by-eleven feet and were reported to bring in public revenues of up to $2.5 million.

In June 1992, CWLC decided to revisit the billboard issue out of its concern that most of the existing billboards advertised alcohol and tobacco and seemed to be located predominantly in poor communities of color. It chose to target Penn Advertising, a local billboard company that owned most of Baltimore's larger billboards.

The Coalition approached Councilwoman Sheila Dixon, a strong ally, to introduce legislation banning billboards for alcohol and tobacco to the Baltimore City Council. The legislation hit a snag, however, when

City Solicitor Neal Janey ruled that, while the tobacco billboards could be handled locally, the state had preemptory powers on the alcohol issue. So the Coalition split the bill and sought an author in the state legislature for legislation that would enable alcohol billboards to be handled as a local issue. Kevin Jordan, CWLC organizer described that process:

> When we started [proposing] the bill no one even took it seriously....We introduced the bill to state legislators and people kind of patted us on the head and said, "Oh, that's nice." And that was it. Our first person who was going to introduce it, didn't introduce it. We had to get someone else.[28]

CWLC began its effort with help and training from the Citizens Planning and Housing Association, first-term senator Ralph Hughes, and Amy Blank, chief lobbyist for Advocates for Children. Early on, the group attended a legislative day sponsored by Advocates for Children, where Coalition members had a chance to meet with state legislators, called delegates in Maryland. Attending the session taught members that they would have to make a powerful show of community support, since they were pushing controversial legislation that was likely to involve high-powered, highly paid lobbyists from the alcohol and tobacco industries. According to Jordan:

> The delegates said, "You have to get your people active, it can't be just your leaders talking. It has to be everybody." Phone calls and letters were very important, they said. Letters might be hard to get people to write but the phone call is very easy. It kind of came from that day. People were talking about it. We knew that we had to do something and not everybody would be able to get down to Annapolis every day. But even people who worked would want to be able to do something.[29]

CWLC organized a formidable lobbying assault to get their enabling legislation passed. As the legislation moved from committee to committee, from the Senate to the House, community people lobbied with delegates in person. CWLC's Jordan and Coalition chair Bev Thomas became a constant presence in Annapolis, spending "ten hours a day, five days a week" at the capital. When funding was available, buses were hired to bring the mostly elderly Coalition members in from Baltimore to attend hearings and to lobby. Coalition member Mary Lou Kline remembers how she and other Coalition members were carefully prepared for their first lobbying effort:

A whole group went down and we met in one room and they gave us the bills and a paper that had a synopsis of the bills.... We pretty much talked about how you're just going to talk to them, you're going to point out what these bills are, why we want them, encourage them to try to support us....Different people went to different senators. We were told to try to get them to commit, try to get them to promise to do something.[30]

COMMUNICATING STRENGTH

A phone tree, which became the backbone of the lobbying effort, was one of the many ways in which the Coalition made room for large numbers of people to participate. Kline, a grandmother with caretaking responsibilities for several grandchildren, wanted to be able to contribute to the effort but needed to spend most of her days at home. She became phone tree chairperson. Jordan put together a list of names and numbers culled from CWLC meeting sign-in sheets. To activate the phone tree, Kline would call 12 members, each of those members would call names on their own lists and so on. Often Jordan and Thomas would develop mini-scripts covering the general issues which community people could use when calling. According to Kline,

Bev and Kevin would call me up and say, look, we have got this going, we have this on the line....You have to call these people and tell them to get on the phone. So I would make all these notes and right away start calling these people on the phone and tell them this has happened down at Annapolis, get to your delegate, your senator, whatever.[31]

Kline described a local beauty shop owner whose efforts exemplify the kind of enthusiasm the billboard campaign generated among people, a momentum that was reflected by the high levels of participation on the phone tree.

This one lady in particular runs her own beauty shop. It is difficult for her to come to meetings but I could always call her at work and give her the message. She would make the phone calls. She might not just call her phone tree people. She had customers coming in the shop. She had petitions to sign. She gave them letters....Some of the people, they added people to the phone tree that I don't even know about. That's fine. One lady I know said, "I tell every person I call, now you call ten more people." I'd hear people say, "I call all my family."[32]

Because of this outpouring of grassroots support, the bill was seen as a local, non-controversial matter in the Senate. The bill also had the support of Baltimore Mayor Kurt Schmoke, who sent City Solicitor Neal Janey to testify on its behalf. Opposition came from lobbyists representing the Liquor Board, Distilled Spirits Council, Seagrams and the billboard industry.

At a March 22, 1993, hearing before the Senate Economic Environmental Affairs Committee, both opponents and proponents of the bill turned out in large numbers. When the bill moved to the Senate floor, each of the Baltimore senators was behind it, except for one who abstained from voting. Action mainly centered around exemptions that would allow liquor ads to remain at Oriole Park at Camden Yards (home of the Baltimore Orioles baseball club), Pimlico Race Course and Memorial Stadium. With these amendments, the bill passed with just five dissenting votes (41–5).

BIG GUNS VS. GRANDPARENTS

When the bill moved to the House, Penn Advertising changed its tactics. Instead of lobbying on its own as it did in the Senate, Penn Advertising's director of governmental affairs, Fred Lauer, hired Bruce Bereano, the Tobacco Institute's major lobbyist in Annapolis. CWLC, which had not received much media coverage on the bill (SB 808) up to this point, decided to use this turn of events to its advantage. Jordan recounted the genesis of an April 2, 1993 *Baltimore Sun* article with the headline, "High-Powered Lobbyist Threatens Bill to Ban Liquor Advertising." The article was one of the first to frame the effort as an uphill battle between community people and powerful lobbyists:

> One of the things we were able to do was to get some of the media to couch it as a little guys vs. big guys thing. These big lobbyists are trying to crush the little guys again....The billboard industry hired the top lobbyist in the state midway through the process, Bruce Bereano. He's "the man," the highest-paid lobbyist in the state. That is when we started saying they hired this guy to kill the community's initiative.[33]

Thomas spoke of the impact a subsequent article on Bereano had on the community and how it fed into the organizing efforts of the Coalition:

> When the *Sun* did an article about Bruce Bereano, people said, "Oh, that's the same guy. All that money and stuff." People

latched onto us. That's us against the lobbyists. They make the connections. Every day people became conscious of what the process is. Why we don't get certain things. Opening up to many folks that we don't have legislators down there just doing it for us. It's a whole process. [34]

In the House the bill was sponsored by Elijah Cummings. The Coalition's lobbying efforts had a profound effect on Cummings, who at one point told members that he "felt like his grandparents came up to Annapolis" and held him accountable. He commented, "I've gotten more calls from everyday people in favor of this bill than any other issue. People are saying, 'We want to save our children.'"

Senate Bill 808 came before the House Economic Matters Committee, of which Cummings was vice-chair. Committee Chairman Cas Taylor was taken with CWLC's commitment to improve community conditions. He was also impressed with documentation presented by the Coalition that indicated that certain low-income African-American neighborhoods were being targeted by the liquor industry. The industry lobbyists argued that the bill set a bad precedent, raised First Amendment issues and would have economic ramifications, causing Penn Advertising to lose $2 million in revenue and to lay off 12 of its 53 workers. [35] Furthermore, Bereano argued that the issue should be decided upon by the city council, not the state legislature.

Thomas commented, "It was a real eye-opener, how strong the lobbyists were. The delegates seemed truly trapped. Folks were locked in by alcohol and tobacco dollars." [36]

Taylor came up with an idea for an amendment that would send the bill back to the Baltimore City Council. With that amendment in hand, the bill received a favorable committee report and went to the House floor. Later, as he spoke on the floor, Taylor said that the city was "only being authorized to control its own social destiny." [37]

The struggle continued on the House floor. Attempts at two other amendments to weaken the bill failed. Ed Moehler, head of the state AFL-CIO, put forward the potential job loss argument during legislative hearings. CWLC supporters counter-argued that the job loss potential would be addressed by the phase-in aspect of the bill (allowing contracts to run out before the ban took effect) and that many other products could be advertised on the billboards. As one supporter said, "If it's not liquor, it's Frito-Lay." [38] The final House vote was 75 to 33 in favor of the legislation.

Penn Advertising began a campaign to encourage Governor William Donald Schaeffer to veto the bill. Although Schaeffer had made preventive health a hallmark of his administration, he had a long-standing relationship with the billboard company. A sympathetic government insider let CWLC know that the veto was a real possibility, and encouraged the group to revive its lobbying efforts and focus on a letter-writing campaign to the governor. It worked. Not only did Governor Schaeffer sign the bill on May 27, 1993, he announced his own initiative to phase alcohol and tobacco ads out of Mass Transit Administration buses and replace them with a state-sponsored ad campaign to encourage youth to stay away from those products. The *Baltimore Sun* noted that when the signature came it "capped weeks of frenzied lobbying, with dozens of letters and calls flowing into Mr. Schaeffer's office, some from students calling for a ban and others from billboard workers fearing such a move would cost their jobs." [39]

With the enabling legislation for the alcohol billboard ban in hand, Coalition members headed back to Baltimore and the city council for the next phase of their effort—to pass bills banning both alcohol and tobacco billboards in the city. In retrospect, many felt that what they did at the state level was twice as hard as anything they would do in the city. But the group faced other challenges as the industry introduced new and often unexpected tactics.

The twin bills would not be introduced until September, when the city council opened its 1993 session. Councilwoman Sheila Dixon had introduced legislation dealing with the same issues seven years before as one of her first acts on the council and was ready to be the bills' sponsor.

DRAFTING A BILL TO PASS MUSTER

Drafting legislation that would outlaw the billboards and withstand court challenges was the next task. Through connections at the Citizens Planning and Housing Association (CPHA), the Coalition's umbrella organization, the group was able to line up the assistance of a local law firm, Gallagher, Evelius & Jones. Attorney Christopher J. Fritz, a partner with a background in First Amendment law, headed the team of pro bono lawyers from the firm. In a series of meetings, community members and the legal team hammered out parameters for legislation that would be constitutional and withstand court challenges.

Fritz later reflected upon some of the concerns that shaped the drafting of the legislation: "Since the beginning our concern had been about the billboards themselves and the way they appeal to minors. They are a unique medium. Parents can't intervene and turn them off the way you can a radio or TV ad."[40]

The team constantly thought in terms of the potential legal challenges, including First Amendment challenges, concerning the restriction of commercial free speech. But an additional issue involving federal preemption under the Federal Cigarette Labeling and Advertising Act (FCLA) also needed to be taken into account while drafting the tobacco legislation. FCLA requires that all cigarette packages carry one of four rotating warning messages and prohibits state and local governments from preempting these warnings by creating their own requirements regarding advertising cigarettes based on smoking and health.

Fritz explained that he believes the final drafts of the bills, which restrict all outdoor alcohol and tobacco advertising except in industrial areas and at several large sports facilities including Pimlico Race Course, Memorial Stadium, and Oriole park at Camden Yards, were strong because they focus on a very narrow problem—outdoor advertising. The final versions are persuasive in their arguments, citing U.S. Supreme Court opinions, statements by the U.S. Surgeon General and studies by the governor's Drug and Alcohol Abuse Commission and the state Department of Education to illustrate the damaging effects tobacco and alcohol advertising has on youth.

He added that still another strength of the bills was that, by exempting industrial areas, the group was doing specifically less than it was given permission to do by the state legislature.

> We stepped back from what we could have done....We did this to make absolutely certain that we were within constitutional bounds. And because the problem we were addressing had to do with ads that were affecting children. So it didn't make a lot of sense to say, well, in a business zone or an industrial zone we were going to ban billboards. Because you could make the argument, yeah, kids are going to see them there, but they are also going to see them on interstate highways, which is another exception. But generally speaking, where kids live and go to school and play is in neighborhoods. We wanted to be absolutely sure we were right.[41]

By the time the city council returned from summer recess, Councilwoman Dixon, Council President Mary Pat Clarke, Mayor Kurt Schmoke and at least three other council members were already backing Council Bills 626 and 627 (banning alcohol and tobacco billboards, respectively). Additionally, in response to a request from the city, Attorney General J. Joseph Curran, Jr. wrote an opinion stating that Maryland municipalities had the right to curb tobacco billboards in order to protect minors from pro-smoking messages and to deter sales of cigarettes to youth. A week later, City Solicitor Neal Janey declared that federal and state laws would not preempt either ordinance. Both Janey and Curran stated that while federal and state law prevent local jurisdictions from banning smoking for health reasons, they would allow limits designed to keep youth from purchasing cigarettes.

ORGANIZING FOR THE NEXT PHASE

The Coalition stepped up its organizing and lobbying efforts, meeting with individual city council members and involving the press. Thomas elaborated on some of the methods used by the group:

> This Coalition is not just marching, not just protesting. We're working within the system and we touch base with all levels of the system. We keep in contact with everyone. For one thing, everything we do, we send out communication to the news media. It doesn't have to be a press conference. When we're having our regular meetings, picnics, hearings, any of the reporters can pick it up if they choose to.

She stressed the importance of varying meeting sites, and of trying to reach the community by involving the churches:

> When we meet, we have our meetings in a different part of town each time. We try to have them in a church so that hopefully we will get the minister or the church involved if no more than having them give the invocation....We also have sent letters to ministers throughout the city asking them to do a special sermon. We tried to pick a special time frame for those sermons with the agenda being the issue. One example was the targeting of low-income communities by alcohol and tobacco industries.[42]

Reverend Norman Handy, CWLC co-chair, described the grassroots efforts organized through local churches:

> We were contacting people through our churches. We were passing out petitions [in support of the legislation] as well as cards on Sundays so that people could sign up and send cards and make calls. My church has an average attendance of 170 to 220 people and when we put the petition out, we left it out for three Sundays. Each sheet contained 50 lines for signatures and

we wound up using four and a half sheets for people who would sign up after services. They could also take a pack of postcards for their respective districts. We also had an instruction sheet of who to call, how to call the mayor, the state attorney, the governor. We were flooding them with calls. [43]

At the same time, the opposition stepped up its local efforts. A group called Citizens for Responsible Advertising formed to oppose the alcohol billboard bill. (A coalition to defeat the tobacco bill never developed to the same degree.) Describing its membership as "retailers, employees of the beverage industry and citizens," the group held protest rallies and met with city council members "to suggest other ways to deal with billboards and underage drinking." [44] Spokespeople included Fred Lauer from Penn Advertising and Daisy Jackson, president of the Maryland United Licensed Beverage Association (MULBA), who said, "We believe there is a better way to deal with the problem of underage drinking without putting us out of business." [45]

MEDIA MAKE A DIFFERENCE

With the victory at the state level behind them, the Coalition found that the media, particularly print media, were much more responsive to the billboard issue. Jordan described the group's outreach efforts:

> Nothing is too small to tell. Even if they don't want to print it but you are thinking of them and giving reporters information, that's important. You want to make each station or reporter feel like they're the key writer. It may seem manipulative but it isn't really. It was a little hard for a while with the *Sun* because they kept changing reporters on us so we had to keep going over everything. Some of the other papers had the same reporters, and you just had to take the time to go over the complete history, all the info you have, answer the few questions they have. It's developing relationships....It's the same with anything. You try to make people feel important because people are important. But you don't feel only certain people are important and then the media, they're all dogs. You treat people in the media the way you treat people in your coalitions." [46]

Jordan and Thomas agreed that the media coverage added to the organizing momentum. Thomas explained:

> Wherever I go, folks that I don't know say, "I've seen you someplace." I say, "The billboards," and they say, "You go, girl!" These are people who might say there's not much we can do in

our community. All of a sudden you can see people saying, "Hey, these are some of the problems we are facing and we need to do this." People have become members after hearing us on the radio, after seeing us on television. [47]

While coverage and editorials that appeared in the *Baltimore Sun* added a certain element of credibility to the campaign, the local African-American papers, the *Baltimore Times* and *The Afro-American*, also played a critical role. Ursula Battle, the reporter who covered the bills for *The Afro-American*, provided in-depth coverage and named the billboard issue one of the paper's top ten stories of the year. And the *Baltimore Times* ran in its entirety a statement from the local chapter of the Urban League—an organization that traditionally works on issues concerning poor people—urging that "rather than resolve this concern through a bill, that the community look at this from a non-emotional view and from a factual and economic one." [48] The paper's George Collins was the only newspaper reporter who provided thorough coverage of the controversy.

INDUSTRY TACTICS ATTEMPT TO DIVIDE THE COMMUNITY

The Urban League's position against the bills provides a salient example of the complications that arose when the alcohol industry applied pressure to a well-established community organization with a long history of dependence on industry funding. The Urban League urged negotiation with the industry in its statement:

> The Baltimore Urban League is not interested in losing corporate sponsors, who have been partners in our positive efforts in the community. Further, we believe that if these business leaders are completely apprised of our concerns, they would be empathetic and willing to come to the table and co-develop a common effort that results in resolving the problem of oversaturation of billboards in our community, and the improvement of our relationship. [49]

State delegate Elijah Cummings expressed his extreme disappointment with the Urban League in an article that appeared in the *Baltimore Times*, in which he stated, "Even after the bill was passed and signed into law by the governor, a prominent lobbyist told me, 'We'll find a way to stop it.' Little did I know that the way would be through an organization that has been about lifting up black people." [50]

According to Thomas:

> There was a lot of pain in the sense that for many years in the
> African-American community we have been able to say that a
> lot of our injustices come from the white corporate world. The
> Urban League and the NAACP [which did not take a position
> on the ordinance] were founded because of injustice suf-
> fered…so that those who are disadvantaged would have a fair
> share. But now they were participating in the same system that
> caused them to be founded. Because they were being sponsored
> [by those industries] their hands were tied.[51]

Jordan said that CWLC had not been able to get either the Urban
League or the NAACP to sign on as supporters of the bills. Matthews
Wright, director of community services and allocation for Associated
Black Charities (ABC) and a CWLC member, said that while the bills
were being considered by the city council, representatives from
Anheuser-Busch met with several community groups. ABC itself had
received approximately $10,000 over two years from the company,
mainly in sponsorships for special events. And more than $100,000 had
been given to African-American community groups by Anheuser-
Busch, most of it through the Urban League. Representatives from ABC
met with Anheuser-Busch themselves, although the organization
remained a strong supporter of the Coalition's work. After that meeting,
Wright said, it became clear that Anheuser-Busch was working on its
public image:

> They just wanted to single out organizations, corral them in their
> issue and then go after another one and say these organizations
> support us in their efforts and we're not totally bad guys. But
> no one has said that they were totally bad guys. What is being
> said is that the manner in which they used the proliferation of
> advertising creates an environment within neighborhoods that
> detracts from the stability and aesthetics of that community.[52]

After the Urban League's statement was published, the Coalition
put together a group to meet with Roger Lyons, executive director of
the Urban League, and Rodney Orange and George Bunton of NAACP.
The group included Lenneal Henderson, a board member of both CPHA
and the Urban League, and Leonard Saunders, a CWLC member and
lifetime member of the NAACP. They were unable to get the Urban
League to rescind their statement publicly. But the billboard issue had
generated so much public support that the published statement sparked
a community outcry that took on a life of its own. This may have
contributed to the Urban League's decision to rescind its position quietly.

According to Jordan, Roger Lyons was publicly shamed on numerous occasions:

> On the Morgan State University radio station, people were calling in and saying, "I can't believe you would betray the community like that." This was not a concerted effort on our part to do anything, it was just people's inclination to do something. He got calls in his office all the time. He was in the barber shop one time when people were talking about it, saying the Urban League were traitors.... It was something that generated among itself in the African-American community. [53]

Public consciousness was stirred enough to criticize another industry tactic on November 5, when the *Baltimore Sun* reported that Penn Advertising planned to pull down tobacco and alcohol billboards near schools and churches. The company would paint the red symbol of a child on the first of 111 signs to show none would advertise alcohol or tobacco again. [54] Thomas felt that this was a hollow gesture; Penn Advertising had previously claimed to have a self-imposed policy not to avoid advertise alcohol and cigarettes near churches and schools. She commented:

> The *Sun* did the coverage of when Penn Advertising made the gesture of their press conference on the symbol. That did so much for us in terms of consciousness of the community. Folks were saying "What is that little symbol going to do?" [55]

Although elected officials supporting the billboard legislation called the offer a positive one, they said that it would not stop attempts to pass the legislation. City Council President Mary Pat Clarke was quoted as saying, "It shows that they can do it. I just see this as a positive voluntary movement. Our legislation would complete what they started." [56]

"YES, I CAN DEMAND A CHANGE"—THE PASSAGE OF THE BILLS

By the time the final public hearing on City Council Bills 626 and 627 was held on November 17, 1993, 10 out of 18 city council members were sponsoring the bills, along with city council president Clarke. A crowd of more than 250 people, including academic researchers, health professionals, clergy, residents, and busloads of tavern and liquor store owners, participated in the proceedings, which lasted until 2:30 a.m. CWLC members wore powder-blue T-shirts with their logo in the shape of Maryland that helped to promote unity and to identify them as a group.

The final vote on the alcohol legislation came after the council voted to table a last-minute amendment sponsored by Councilman Wilbur E. Cunningham, one of the bill's opponents. The amendment would have allowed liquor stores to advertise brands and prices in certain restricted areas of the buildings. On December 6, the alcohol bill passed on a vote of 15 to 3 and the council gave final approval at their meeting three days later. On January 6, Mayor Schmoke signed City Council Bill 626 into law.

The vote on the tobacco bill was postponed, partly in response to reports that the Federal Trade Commission was divided over whether it could legally ban cigarette advertising featuring Joe Camel. Federal law strictly prohibited state and local regulation of tobacco advertising if the regulation purports to address tobacco health risks. The Baltimore ordinance had to restrict itself to regulating tobacco ads because of their appeal to youth. Joe Camel ads were already at the center of controversy as the FTC was weighing whether or not the ads had youth appeal. A decision in their favor would strengthen the ordinance. A failure to find Joe Camel ads appealing to youth would hurt the law's standing.

Some advocates felt the case for the bill would also be strengthened after the Surgeon General's report concerning youth and tobacco use was released. The report was slated for publication in early February of that year and would be a comprehensive summary of every federally funded study, survey and report on problems concerning youth and tobacco. This was just the thorough set of findings the Coalition needed to provide a solid legal foundation for the ordinance.

On February 28, amidst the cheers of community leaders and activists, the city council voted unanimously to ban tobacco billboards in residential Baltimore neighborhoods, making the city the first in the nation to take a strong stand against tobacco and alcohol advertising. While the Coalition members sitting in that city council chamber knew court challenges by the tobacco, alcohol and billboard industries were imminent, they also knew that the hardest and most important part of their journey was over. Thomas reflected:

> If nothing else happens out of this whole process other than tapping the hearts and the thinking of everyday people, I think we will consider it a success. Somewhere down the line all the things we are learning and passing on to other folks can be used in the future. Not necessarily in the same format but it can be used to give folks the courage to say, "Yes, I can demand

a change. Yes, I can make a change, even if I have never done it before."[57]

Final Thoughts

For both coalitions, community organizing and resident participation was key. They were both pitted against powerful interests but they were able to prevail with "people power," by bringing large numbers of concerned residents into the process to pressure decisionmakers. Building a strong, democratic base was the most important priority of these campaigns. Without such a base, there can be no long-term, effective change.

Neither group got too caught up in the regulatory process. They organized participation in the process without "becoming the process" itself. In other words, they avoided jargon, prepared residents to participate on their own terms and tell their own stories. They stayed focused on their organizing goals and were not seduced into abandoning their organizing work by their access to public officials. It is all too common for groups to ask members or allies to write letters or make phone calls without involving them in the process of identifying demands, testimony or meeting with public officials. Groups that don't develop avenues for meaningful grassroots involvement are soon isolated and rendered ineffective, as members fade away out of apathy and mistrust.

Although these coalitions were committed to developing grassroots leadership and organizing principles, they also effectively used "experts" (researchers, attorneys, bureaucrats and others) to help shape and inform their strategy. Both groups developed an impressive array of expert volunteers and consultants and convened them both in groups and in individual meetings as part of their own research process. In particular, pro bono lawyers played a critical role in the policy process. In each case it was the coalition that determined their relationship with these experts as well as how any information gathered with their help would be used.

Thanks to the work of CCSAPT and CWLC (among others), grassroots efforts to regulate alcohol outlets and outdoor advertising of alcohol and tobacco are spreading nationally. By 1998, more than 90 cities had enacted restrictive alcohol outlet or billboard ordinances, or both. Communities are also taking on industry sponsorships of cultural festivals, tobacco promotion (i.e., cigarette giveaways and concert sponsorships) and more.

Cinco de Mayo festivals, in particular, have been fertile ground for grassroots activism to "take back the culture" from these industries. The results of these efforts, as documented in the brilliant research of Dr. Maria Alaniz, include fundamental shifts away from domination by alcohol and tobacco in both festival policies *and* community leadership. "Old guard" leadership, traditionally operating as allies and ambassadors for these industries, has been challenged—and often displaced—by activists committed to a more contentious relationship with these industries.

As a result, alcohol and tobacco industries are not simply flashing potential contributions and expecting community leadership to offer up their festivals. Cigarette give-aways have all but disappeared and alcohol service and promotion—when allowed at all—are much more restricted. The new atmosphere at these events is attracting families and helping to break the association between the celebrations and alcohol and tobacco promotion.[58]

These local community victories have forced the alcohol and tobacco industries to turn to the state and federal arena for relief. Unfortunately, industry interests have prevailed in the passage of a few state and federal ordinances. However, activists are fighting back and continuing to advance legislative agendas of their own.

For example, CSSAPT joined forces with the California Council on Alcohol Policy to develop statewide muscle to fight alcohol industry initiatives. The attention to state issues is paying off: most alcohol industry initiatives in California were either defeated outright or amended to reverse their intended impact.

There are also some important lessons here with regard to the potency of framing for institutional accountability. Both of these campaigns focused on institutional actors—not individual behavior—as the target for change. By emphasizing better government regulation and clear written policies, both organizations created a strong regulatory framework upon which they could build toward greater institutional accountability. Cutting the issue in this way also provided clear, easy-to-understand organizing handles that engaged community folk because it gave them a considerable "hammer" for addressing these issues on a larger scale.

MAKING MORE PIE:

Local Initiatives that Increase Resources and Institutional Accountability

> They would throw a crumb here and a crumb there and say
> "Split this little 'pie' between all these people." Everyone was so
> busy fighting over the crumbs that we almost forgot we could
> make more "pie"—if we could just get into the pantry.
>
> —ANONYMOUS ACTIVIST ON LOCAL FUNDING FOR YOUTH PROGRAMS IN OAKLAND, CA

> We have always known that heedless self-interest was bad morals;
> we now know that it is bad economics.
>
> —FRANKLIN D. ROOSEVELT [1]

If the Roosevelt Administration ushered in the era of the New Deal for working people, it was the Reagan Administration that forged a New Deal for business. "Deregulation" became the operative word. Cutbacks in occupational safety regulations, labor standards, water safety and food inspections were justified by the increased profit that cuts in cost would bring. Greed was good. Need was bad. And the idea of the corporation as a community citizen (though always difficult to implement and enforce) was replaced with that of the corporation as "individual," with all of the rights and none of the responsibilities.

As discussed in Chapter 1, corporations have a major impact on health and quality of life. Policies that regulate or deregulate companies affect our tax base, our wages, our access to health care, our public health and safety, and our natural resources. Although not always considered within the realm of public health, initiatives that force corporate accountability are at the heart of improving the fundamental risk factors for health status in communities. These initiatives have made a significant contribution to community health and well-being. Initiatives that address wages, work conditions and environmental justice appear to have the greatest potential impact.

Governments themselves are also important engines for economic development and employment. In New Mexico, for example, one out of four people is employed in the public sector. Similarly, Alaska has 27 percent public-sector employment and Wyoming 26 percent. Nationally, 15 percent of those not employed on farms are working for some branch of government, and usually with better benefits than their private-sector counterparts.[2] Public budget priorities and investments have a profound impact on any local economy. Therefore, advocates cannot ignore public institutions in their efforts to address community development, job opportunities, and residents' quality of life.

This chapter explores initiatives that seek to gain concrete changes in the way both companies and local governments do business. Living-wage campaigns leverage the public contracts process to win higher wages and more rights for workers in their area. Other initiatives seek to apply public incentives or disincentives to force the private sector to control pollution, or slow corporate relocation or downsizing. Also included is an example of a youth-led initiative to reorder city funding priorities so that more of existing public monies will be spent on local youth programs and employment. Each initiative represents innovative ways of addressing basic, quality-of-life issues through local policymaking.

Living-Wage Campaigns

"Living-wage" laws have been enacted or are under consideration in counties and cities across the country. In contrast to the federal minimum-wage law, which can only be set by federal legislation, local living-wage ordinances set clear standards for minimum allowable wages that are indexed to the local cost of living and to inflation. Some proposals focus only on raising wages, while others include mandates for insurance benefits and "right to organize" (i.e., join trade unions) clauses for low-wage workers. Living-wage proposals are designed to raise the wages of very-low-income workers by requiring state or municipal contractors, and business recipients of public subsidies or tax breaks, to set minimum salaries so that wages provide at least enough income to keep a family of four at or above the poverty line.

As the low-wage service sector of the economy expands, more and more working people do not earn enough to take care of their basic needs. Unfortunately, it is often the economic policies of public agencies that create these conditions, including public subsidies, marketing programs and the like that seek to expand historically low-wage industries in tourism and retail; privatization of work contracts; and the failure of public agencies to develop adequate public transportation to locations where higher-wage jobs are created.

The living-wage strategy seeks to hold government accountable for its roles as regulator, economic engine, and agent of the public interest. Its premise, the living wage, harks back to the old union cry, "A full day's pay for a full day's work!" except this time, the bosses being called on are elected by the workers—a difference that this strategy fully exploits. Here are some examples:

In Boston, a diverse coalition of trade union organizations, the Association of Community Organizations for Reform Now (ACORN), and other neighborhood groups moved the city council to pass a living-wage ordinance in 1997 requiring companies getting city contracts or subsidies (of a significant amount) to pay their employees $7.70 per hour. The wage is the minimum amount required to keep a family of four above poverty. The measure also includes provisions for hiring city residents, mandates companies seeking city funds to report on job creation and wages, and creates an advisory board on city assistance with seats for labor and ACORN representatives.

In Santa Clara County, California (home to Silicon Valley, an international center for the high-tech industry), the county board of supervisors passed a law in 1995 requiring manufacturing firms applying for tax abatements to report the number of jobs to be created and the firms' wage rates and benefits and to disclose any other subsidies they are seeking. Businesses receiving an abatement must pay a minimum wage of $10.00 per hour and provide health insurance or a suitable alternative to all permanent employees. The measure gives the county a money-back guarantee if goals are not met. This effort received strong trade union participation from the South Bay AFL-CIO Labor Council. The California Budget Project, a research and policy advocacy group, and Working Partnerships USA also played leading roles. This alliance demonstrates the potential for effective collaboration among community groups, trade unions and policy research and advocacy groups.

Other cities with such laws include San Jose and New York City, where city contractors must pay employees union-scale wages. Milwaukee, Oakland, New Haven and Jersey City, New Jersey are among the cities that have enacted ordinances that require city contractors to pay employees a living wage as determined for their respective areas.[3]

BALTIMORE PROVES LIVING WAGE WORKS

As with any local policy, the first living-wage ordinances were the toughest to pass. Once the precedent was set, the work became much easier (though not easy). Baltimore provided an early precedent by enacting one of the nation's first living-wage ordinances.

Baltimoreans United in Leadership Development (BUILD), a community organization affiliated with the Industrial Areas Foundation, and the American Federation of State, County and Municipal Employees (AFSCME), organized the Solidarity Sponsoring Committee (SSC) to campaign for a living-wage ordinance. SSC was comprised primarily of low-wage service workers living in the Baltimore area, many of whom were involved in local faith institutions from which BUILD draws a great deal of its base.

The ordinance was initiated out of BUILD's concerns for low-wage earners, who, despite their full-time jobs, still required agency support for food, housing and other services. Church leaders who administered many of these aid programs were disturbed that employment was not making a real difference in these workers' lives. BUILD's research on the problem showed that these poverty-wage jobs were mostly in business sectors subsidized by city money. Two primary sectors involved in this phenomenon were the expanding downtown retail sector, where low-wage jobs were being created, and the private-sector contracts that were taking over city government jobs. Since both these areas of job creation were funded by city money and were a result of city policy, the SSC went to the city council to get some minimum protections enacted for this growing segment of workers.

The law that was passed mandated a minimum hourly wage of $6.10 per hour for anyone working on a city service contract starting July 1, 1995, with the wage increasing to $6.60 per hour for contracts signed after July 1, 1996. The ordinance further stipulated that the wage be increased annually, upon the approval of Baltimore's Board of Estimates, until it equals the amount required to support a family of four above the federal poverty line. The wage was scheduled to meet that minimum by 1999; subsequently it will be indexed to inflation.

The ordinance establishes a mechanism for enforcement and imposes significant penalties on contractors in violation. Contractors are required to submit payrolls on a biweekly basis to the Wage Commission and can be fined $10.00 per day for each day their payrolls are late. Noncompliant service contractors are liable for fines and back pay to underpaid employees. Violators can also lose their eligibility for city contracts for a year and be barred from bidding for up to three years if they are found to be noncompliant on more than three contracts in a two-year period. Companies can receive extensions of their pre-ordinance pay scale ranging from one to four years. After the extension period is over, they are to phase in the wage rate in effect when the contract was awarded.

Opponents claim that a living-wage law will cause increases in the costs of public contracts and lead to unemployment and an unfavorable local business climate. A study by The Preamble Center for Public Policy on Baltimore's living-wage law has found that these charges are groundless. And given that Baltimore's ordinance is, in many ways, typical of the many living-wage proposals and laws being enacted around the nation, the study offers important insights for the movement nationally.

Preamble Center found that, instead of raising the cost of public contracts in Baltimore, the real cost of city contracts has actually decreased since the ordinance went into effect. There was no decrease in job availability, either, as no companies interviewed as part of the study (of those holding contracts before and after the ordinance's enactment) reported reducing staffing levels because of the higher wage requirements. Charges that the ordinance would be too expensive to implement were also rebutted, as Preamble Center found the cost to taxpayers was a mere 17 cents per person annually. Although there was a slight decline in the average numbers of bids per contract, the study found no effect on the competitiveness of the bidding process. Overall, the study could find no evidence that living wage hurt Baltimore's business climate in any way. The authors concluded, "There is no evidence that businesses have responded negatively to the passage of the ordinance. In fact, the value of business investment in the City of Baltimore actually increased substantially in the year after passage of the law."[4]

ACORN BUILDS NATIONAL MOVEMENT
FOR LOCAL LIVING WAGE

ACORN is building a national movement around local living-wage ordinances as a way of strategically leveraging the local policymaking process into concrete victories for low-income people. The group is undoubtedly one of the most influential organizations (along with labor union councils) in the movement for a living wage. ACORN is leading campaigns by several local chapters while providing technical assistance to at least a dozen others whose campaigns are in various stages of development.

The Living-wage campaign is a natural outgrowth of ACORN's nearly thirty years of work for economic justice. The organization was founded in Little Rock, Arkansas as an experiment by the National Welfare Rights Organization (NWRO) to build broader support for its cause. A group of mothers on welfare formed ACORN's first membership in 1970. It soon mushroomed into a national organization of active local chapters. ACORN's focus is on the development of diverse local organizing initiatives that engage a broad cross-section of low- and moderate-income people. Given its commitment to economic justice, bread-and-butter issues drive ACORN's work.

The organization has waged various campaigns ranging from fighting for traffic lights to benefits for low-wage workers and organizing farmers to stop a utility company from building a coal-burning plant near their lands. All of these campaigns focused on the needs of those of low and moderate income and were framed in such a way that their target was the most accessible decisionmaker, the one from whom groups had the greatest chance of gaining concessions.

This pragmatic, grassroots organizing led ACORN into the local policy arena early on. Local chapters researched and leveraged existing ordinances to back up demands, introduced some new local ordinances, identified opportunities to increase local authority in governance and therefore their access to authority, and even ran candidates for various offices with some success. As with the coalitions described in Chapter 2, local government made an ideal target for ACORN's efforts: the officials and the offices were more accessible, it was easier to organize strong numbers for local response, and these institutions were, at least in theory, accountable to their constituents.

ACORN began its foray into public-sector jobs policy with its "First Source" campaign in 1980. First Source ordinances (or in some cases, agreements) required developers to hire low-income residents directly from the city where they were building. According to Jenn Kern, a member of ACORN's national staff, the initiative grew out of residents' concerns that city monies were subsidizing these developments but residents from surrounding suburbs were being hired for the jobs that resulted.

Kern said, "We had neighborhood meetings [in Boston] where people would talk about going by these new job sites... and they'd say, 'You look at the license plates and they're all from Cambridge instead of Boston or they're all from outside.' First Source was ACORN's first attempt to get at that issue."[5]

By the early 1980s, ACORN's efforts got First Source ordinances or agreements enacted in Miami, Washington, D.C., Bridgeport, Pittsburgh, Dallas, St. Louis, Little Rock and Des Moines. Several other cities developed local-resident hiring programs as well. However, cities were administering these programs (including First Source) without adequate staffing and with lax enforcement. It was clear that much more had to be done.

It was also clear that there were problems beyond simple unemployment. It was becoming increasingly difficult for working families to make ends meet. Residents with jobs found themselves in need of food stamps, Medicare, housing subsidies and other services simply in order to survive. Some workers with full-time jobs still could not afford to keep a roof over their heads. Many of them lived as long-term "guests" in the homes of family members (called "doubling up") while others had nowhere to turn but shelters or the streets. Despite analysts' rosy pronouncements in the media that unemployment was down and stocks were up, regular folk had the sense that something was going wrong.

"There was the reality of the economy in our neighborhoods—the stagnating wages at the lower end [of the pay scale]," Kern recalls. "The only available jobs are these lower wage jobs....Also, the fact that CEOs' salaries were rising and [company] profits were high. It was a natural extension of our work to, in some places, say, 'How is economic development good if it's not translating into good jobs for the people who live there?'"[6]

Fighting for living-wage ordinances was a logical choice for an organization that had both worked in the local policy arena and organized low-wage workers for more than 20 years. Living wage was, as Kern described, "an institutional handle" for dealing with these issues. Their first living-wage initiative was launched in 1997 in St. Paul, where local ACORN members felt they had the resources and the opportunity to gain a victory. St. Paul has a long history of progressive politics—not just through ACORN, but as an organizing hub of trade union activity, corporate accountability work and more. The ACORN chapter there had strong ties with local labor unions and neighborhood groups and there were sympathetic city council members to help move the ordinance.

ACORN decided to put the issue directly to the voters with a ballot measure that would require companies getting public subsidies to pay employees at least $7.21 per hour. A high-powered opposition campaign led by the chamber of commerce outspent supporters about ten to one, and the initiative was narrowly defeated. Yet all the publicity and public awareness generated by the campaign paid off. In its wake the city councils of both St. Paul and Minneapolis formed a joint task force to draft a living-wage ordinance for their respective jurisdictions. In 1997, each of the two city councils passed a law requiring companies that receive more than $100,000 in subsidies to pay $8.25 per hour. The Minneapolis ordinance extends this requirement to all companies receiving contracts from the city.

The Twin Cities experience offered plenty of lessons for the other living-wage campaigns shaping up at the time. For one, they learned in working with labor that it was important to exempt building trades that already had such mechanisms as prevailing wage in construction. Also, most campaigns went directly to the local city council or governing body to win the ordinance. Still, ACORN and its coalition partners always saw these initiatives as grassroots campaigns first and foremost. Their efforts incorporated public hearings, big rallies, yard signs, petition drives and other popular events that put the focus on popular education around economics and building grassroots power—not high-level negotiation with policymakers.[7]

Of course, coalitions had to develop research and other materials to support the initiatives. Groups investigated local contracts, talked to workers and other sources to find glaring illustrations of how the current system wasn't benefiting residents. Working in partnership with national staff and drawing on the work of national policy organizations such as the Center for Budget Priorities and the Economic Policy Institute, coalitions developed local data on poverty and wages to demonstrate the need for the ordinance. One strategy was to contrast the group's living wage demands with what the research revealed were minimum requirements for basic needs—the group's demands were usually conservative by comparison.[8]

All of this information was necessary in order to shift the focus of the debate away from what the ordinance would cost businesses to the burdens on workers and on social services that were ultimately required to subsidize company wages.

The research required hard work, as local governments do little monitoring of contracts—particularly with respect to how contractors treat or compensate employees. Often, staff and members needed to make cold calls to government staffers or file Freedom of Information Act requests to get to the information. Some coalitions, like the Los Angeles Living Wage Coalition, got their city council to fund a more elaborate study. In some cases, coalitions simply partner with supportive researchers to compile the information. At the national level, lawyer groups like Legal Aid Foundation and the National Lawyers Guild and ACORN's own legal defense organization assist with legal research and ordinance review.

From the beginning, ACORN saw the campaigns as an opportunity to deepen ties with labor unions. According to Kern, they never went forward with any living-wage campaign unless they had the strong support of labor unions:

> The most exciting thing about this living-wage campaign has been the way we're building these relationships between our membership and labor....To see these campaigns where you have the heads of Central Labor Councils putting their arms around our board presidents and saying, "Here we are together." In Boston, for example, we forged a coalition that was so strong that it got to the point that we created a coalition that stood up for each other and at the same time deepened the respect of their members and our members toward each other.[9]

For the unions, these campaigns provided needed opportunities to raise visibility and build public support, combined with winning concrete victories for working people. According to Kern, union clout has made the difference, as these campaigns often target local elected officials who depend on labor's vote to get re-elected. ACORN members, who have traditionally worked in low-wage, unorganized jobs, are also learning the value of unions. Kern said,

> We've been able to form these coalitions that have been able to do more together than they would have been able to do alone. And we have also deepened the understanding in the neighborhoods among our membership of the utility of unions.[10]

As a result of these ties, the coalitions have explored ways to incorporate union organizing "handles" in the ordinances, including requiring companies to demonstrate "friendly labor relations" (such as providing unions with access to workers on site) as a qualification for city subsidies. The Los Angeles ordinance, for example, includes a provision that the living wage can be superseded by a mutually agreed upon clause in a collective bargaining agreement. Thus, the ordinance builds in ways of strengthening the power of organized labor in the workplace.

For activists interested in taking up a living-wage campaign Kern advises,

> It's more than passing the ordinance. Think of it as a tool, a step, a piece of a larger thing; a way of increasing and deepening the understanding of these issues around wage stagnation, public monies to foster poverty wages and labor unions. It's a way to increase the strength of the organizations that are in the best position to build power for low-income and working people. In neighborhoods that's community organizations; in the workplace that's unions. [11]

As more cities pass or contemplate living-wage ordinances, ACORN finds itself spending more time on improving provisions and ensuring adequate enforcement. Of course, there are setbacks and problems, including privatizing of public work contracts, competition with low workfare wages and expanding the reach of the policy beyond the public sector.

Ordinances are a result of negotiation and compromise. Therefore, the more precedents are built by ordinances that have passed, the stronger the position of advocates to pass stronger laws. Oakland's ordinance, for example, passed in April, 1998, featured a wider range of provisions than any living-wage law passed previously, including extending the wage to its nonprofit agencies and its redevelopment agency, and the requirement that the city provide health benefits or higher cash compensation in lieu of coverage. Boston's ordinance, passed in 1997, requires that companies declare up front what they'll offer for wages and benefits as part of the bidding process. This way, residents can see if there will be "real jobs" as a result of the city contracting with or subsidizing a company.

Since organizing (not writing laws) is ACORN's first priority, it is using living-wage campaigns as an opportunity to build strong coalitions around issues of economic justice—coalitions that can go beyond passing the ordinance to grappling with the challenges of welfare-to-work, fair housing and other issues facing low-income and working people.

"We have to think of these campaigns as ways to actually build understanding and power, not just win a piece of legislation," said Kern. "Then, we can build a permanent coalition with people who really understand that we need to move on to face welfare/workfare; to face these right-to-organize issues…that this is going somewhere."[12]

Uniting Environment and Development: The Louisiana Green Scorecard

The 85-mile stretch of land along the Mississippi River between Baton Rouge and New Orleans presents a stark contrast in rich and poor. On the one hand, a "who's who" of Fortune 500 petroleum, paper, chemical, and other manufacturing facilities dot the landscape. On the other, the predominantly black communities of this area are among the state's unhealthiest and most impoverished.

It wasn't that way when the first settlers moved into the area. The names of small communities tell of the optimism the early settlers felt when they carved out a life for themselves here, names like Good Hope and Convent. Today, the name given to this stretch of land is more ominous: Cancer Alley.

Giant industries lured to Louisiana by the abundance of natural resources and cheap labor set up operation in the late 1940s and early 1950s. The state provided generous tax breaks and incentives and disregarded the environmental and social cost of these industries. State officials' primary goal was to retain employment; environmental concerns were a distant second. And with a steady flow of campaign contributions to state legislators and threats of job loss to workers and communities if regulations were imposed, these industries maintained their dominance. In 1990, that changed.

A coalition of 25 civil rights groups, labor unions, teachers and tenants groups and environmental organizations, with the help of a sympathetic college professor and a state environmental official, succeeded in pushing through a policy that tied the environmental performance of companies to the tax breaks they received. Thus was born the Louisiana Green Scorecard. The groups had united under the umbrella of the Louisiana Coalition for Tax Justice. It was a textbook example of grassroots organizing, direct action, building coalitions across issue areas, and utilizing strategic research to advance progressive legislation.

Although the legislation was poorly enforced and ultimately reversed after a new administration was elected a year later, it had succeeded in pressuring companies to invest in new pollution-prevention equipment. As a result, more jobs were created, and air pollution and toxic emissions were reduced by 177 million pounds (or more than one-third) over a one-year period. Perhaps the main benefit of the legislation and the campaign to get it enacted was the sense of power it provided to the traditionally disenfranchised people who participated. As organizer Zack Nauth explained, "It's now a lot easier to get people to act and respond to things than it was before. The legislation may have been overturned, but the experience we received is priceless."[13]

CAMPAIGN FOR THE SCORECARD

The campaign to end environmental and economic exploitation in Cancer Alley began long before the enactment of the Green Scorecard. For years, a number of small but vocal and often underfunded grassroots organizations had fought the licensing of toxic facilities in low-income communities and communities of color in the region. In 1989, with the help of national environmental groups, these organizations organized the first "Toxics March."

The march was the culmination of years of work sparked in large measure in 1986, when Professor Oliver Houck of the Tulane University Law School produced a study of Louisiana tax breaks to the petrochemical industry. Houck found that though these companies received 80 percent of the tax exemptions, they created only 15 percent of all the jobs in the state. During one year, two-thirds of the tax breaks went to firms that had violated environmental laws; their tax reductions were 10 times the amount of fines assessed.

Houck's study was a catalyst for groups who had spent years fighting the industries. Together they formed the Louisiana Coalition for Tax Justice to build on the study by pressuring the state and to force the chemical industry to pay its fair share of taxes and cut the amount of pollution it released. The coalition dubbed the campaign a fight against the state's "wealth-fare" system for corporations.

The campaign tapped into Louisiana's deep populist traditions and offered a solution for a state still struggling from the oil bust of the

1980s: make the rich pay their fair share of taxes, use the money to rebuild communities, and penalize, rather than reward polluters. The coalition's first order of business was to gather a broad coalition of people affected by the state's tax breaks to businesses. Next, the group began to build upon Houck's research.

"We took what we learned from Houck and took three years to do a study of our own," reported Mary Faucheaux, former executive director of the Coalition.[14]

The result was a 266-page book called *The Great Louisiana Tax Giveaway* exposing the fallacies in the state's system of tax exemptions. The study found that the state's $2.5 billion in tax breaks, over a three-year period, went to major polluting industries which, rather than expand the number of jobs as the tax breaks intended, had in fact cut their payrolls by 8,000 workers. Only 11 percent of the projects receiving tax exemptions created as many as 10 jobs; one-third added no jobs. And, the study found, nearly all the tax breaks went to existing plants for expansion or routine maintenance. Only six percent went to companies building new plants.

The group pointed out that schools were losing $100 million a year through tax breaks that were fueling education budget deficits and teacher layoffs.

The Toxics March brought public attention to these issues. "We coordinated a 20-city tax caravan through the state to announce the publication of our book and to distribute it," said Faucheaux. "It was also a way to build allies and bring in groups who traditionally didn't organize around labor or environmental issues....During the tour, we gave free copies of our book to school board members, mayors, council members, and legislators. We wanted them to look at the [tax] revenue we were losing and see the impact of these tax breaks on people's lives."[15]

The march, from Baton Rouge to New Orleans was reminiscent of civil rights marches that had occurred in the state years before. The protesters' message was often met with skepticism by state officials who held that the tax exemptions given to industries benefited the state. Moreover, these officials maintained that the various diseases that affected families in these areas were the product of diet and genes rather than pollution. Local and state governments insisted that the tax breaks given to industries were pivotal in attracting business and that any change in this situation would result in massive job loss and plant relocation.

As a result of the march and the research, however state senator

Cleo Fields introduced legislation to remove school taxes from the list of tax exemptions companies enjoyed. Citizen lobbying helped spearhead the bill through committee, but it died on the senate floor. Despite this setback, Paul Templet, then head of the state Department of Environmental Quality (DEQ), designed a scorecard to compare the amount of a company's tax exemption to the amount of its chemical emissions and the number of workers on its payroll by giving each a monetary value or "score."

HOW THE POLICY WORKED

The Louisiana Green Scorecard attempted to combine both development and environmental goals into a single tax measure. The Scorecard was designed to "distribute tax incentives for economic development based on the applying firms' contributions to the quality of life in the state, measured in both economic and environmental terms."[16] The Scorecard can be adapted to any state that offers tax incentives to firms for economic development.

In Louisiana, companies normally received tax benefits under the Industrial Property Tax Exemption Program. There were also other state sales-tax exemptions on building supplies and equipment. The Scorecard ranked companies applying for tax exemptions on a scale of 50 to 100, with 100 meaning that the company would have the least negative impact on the environment and they would agree to hire at least a minimum number of residents. A score of 100 would allow a company the full tax exemption. Any other score entitled a company to receive a percentage of the tax exemption equal to their score.

When the measure was opposed by the state Department of Economic Development, the Louisiana Coalition for Tax Justice fought the department head on. Learning of the application of one company that had omitted any mention of its fine for a large chemical spill while applying for a tax exemption, the Coalition organized demonstrations, sparking a series of agency meetings and more than 200 news articles in state and local papers.

On a separate front, Robert Kuehn of the Public Law Center and the Tulane Environmental Law Clinic—while communicating with Templet—filed a rulemaking request with the department on behalf of 12 public-interest organizations, among them the League of Women Voters, Common Cause, the Sierra Club, the Louisiana Wildlife Federation and the Orleans Audubon Society. A rulemaking request could force the department to develop a policy if it was proven that the state had a duty to have one. Kuehn based the request on both the Louisiana Constitution and State Supreme Court decisions that established that the state's natural resources must be "protected, conserved, and replenished." State law and case history asserted the state government's "affirmative duty" to carry out these protections, which meant tax-exemption grants could not be automatic, but were subject to an environmental review.

The protests, news coverage, legal advocacy and research by the Coalition led to the establishment of a task force to study implementation of the Scorecard. The Governor's Task Force (with Templet as one of the members) drafted the actual policy which was unanimously approved by the state Board of Commerce and Industry Board within the Department of Economic Development.

Though the policy was never fully enforced, it succeed in cutting the amount of pollution in the state and increasing the number of jobs by tying environmental performance to tax breaks. In 1992 the new governor, Edwin W. Edwards, abolished the Scorecard. Still, organizers say the experience has changed the way the state does business.

The campaign demonstrated the importance of proactively defining community needs and undercutting the old argument that communities must choose between good jobs and a clean environment. Although extensive research was an essential part of the process, the Coalition's relative success depended on redefining the issues and focusing on building widespread support for what was an extremely tough battle against high-powered interests.

Youth Get Oakland to Put Kids First

The Kids First! Coalition is a diverse group of youth, adults and community organizations that sought to shift Oakland's public policy from approaches that punish youth to policies that engage youth as partners, utilizing youth development. They decided to shape their campaign as a ballot measure to take their case directly to the city voters. They believed they had more of a shot with sympathetic voters—most of whom were parents—than with a recalcitrant city council that just "didn't get" the notion of youth development.

How Oakland came to having punitive youth policies is a study in the tragic effects of urbanization and corporate and government divestment. As in many cities, the city council was trying to cope with big demographic shifts with few resources—and they were coping very badly.

Oakland, California was once a booming manufacturing town. Residents literally came from all over the world to take advantage of the jobs in this temperate, relatively tolerant working-class city that sat quietly across the bay from San Francisco. People from Asia, the Americas and the U.S. South settled side-by-side in various waves of immigration dating back more than 100 years. By the 1960s, however, whites began to flee to nearby suburbs. In 1966, the wealthy, all-white neighborhood of Piedmont actually seceded from Oakland (establishing a separate city completely surrounded by Oakland) so that it could segregate its lucrative tax base from the city. By 1970, Oakland's population was mostly African American, with growing Latino and Asian communities.

Companies began to leave Oakland as well, and economic divestment took a severe toll on the city. Supermarkets, banks and other services shut down. The unemployed rate steadily climbed while the tax base for local services shrank. By 1985, Oakland was facing an economic crisis made worse by the city's decision to spend millions of dollars in a failed and ill-conceived lawsuit to force the Raiders football team to return to the city after relocating to Los Angeles.

Then there was crack.

As in other areas with high unemployment, crack cocaine hit Oakland hard in the 1980s. As with most drugs, problems came not from the drug's use but from the drug dealing. By 1990, Oakland had one of the highest per capita murder rates in the country. Many of the victims and perpetrators were young people under 25 who were caught in the crossfire of the lucrative crack trade—a "business" that appeared to bring more jobs and capital to Oakland's inner city than had any previous economic development program. It was a dangerous business. Turf wars between rival factions took the form of drive-by shootings, car bombs and random "sprays," in which gunmen simply discharged automatic weapons all over a rival's known area in order to keep everyone in the neighborhood from coming outside.

Yet, ironically, crack also transformed Oakland's economy. Unlike other illicit drugs that came before it, crack displaced the older generation of organized crime syndicates with younger, more entrepreneurial dealers nationwide. Young people—some not even 18 years old—ran large networks of drug distribution and processing rings. Young African-American men were likely recruits into a system that extended its profits into investment in legal enterprises like athletic stores, pager sales and alcohol outlets. In the late 1980s, agency providers in Oakland reported that hundreds of the city's young men and women were employed in the crack trade as dealers, processors, or "lookouts" for street dealers. It was commonplace for ministers to issue pulpit calls at the drug-related funerals urging the growing number of young entrepreneurs to quit the trade and end the violent competition.

Despite the fact that those involved in the drug trade were a small minority of Oakland's youth, all the youth of the city suffered under increased police activity, including random searches and other punitive practices that made youth in Oakland feel like they were living under martial law. Instead of focusing on the fundamental issues of opportunity, employment, enrichment and education, local policymakers turned to more punitive actions like curfews and crackdowns on cruising. Young people became tired of being victims of bad policies and getting blamed for their outcomes. Even kids who were involved in drug dealing began responding to "pulpit calls" and other forms of outreach. They wanted to quit the trade but were faced with a real dilemma: How else could they make a decent living?

Faced with the combination of scapegoating, police harassment, and the decline in services and public schools (Oakland's schools had a reputation for bad management and poor outcomes), young people moved to take more direct action to fight back.

At first, protests were scattered among several groups ranging in politics from the radical Young Comrades to less ideological young members of youth-serving agencies. Together, the groups pushed the debate about "what to do with the youth" to a different level. The city council could no longer operate without considering youth input—young people were in the room and in their face, making a strong case as they shared the litany of issues they faced: There wasn't much for young people to do in the city. Much of the school playground equipment was deemed so unsafe that it was made off-limits by yellow police banners. Recreation center programming was spotty and inconsistent. It was clear that there wasn't enough money being invested in young people's development, yet the city was ready to invest more funds in measures treating youth like criminals, including applying detention and curfews. And as many of the youth would say to the mayor in tense, televised council sessions: "We want to know what's up with that?"

TIME TO STOP BEGGING

Youth working with adults were able to beat back the curfew. However, a small group of youth and youth-serving agencies wanted to go further and push the city to set different priorities with regard to young people. They were tired of being in the position of having to advocate constantly for what were necessary policies and programs. At the center of their efforts was a desire to bring the voice and concerns of young people to the policy arena, to build youth power so that young people had real input in the decisions that affected their lives.

In early 1994, youth members of People United for a Better Oakland (PUEBLO) and the East Bay Asian Youth Center (EBAYC) decided that it was important to ask young people what they thought about violence—and what to do about it.

In surveying more than 1,000 youth throughout Oakland, they found that most kids had experienced some aspect of violence. Perhaps most important, the youth surveyed had very clear ideas about what to do about the problem. They wanted safe, supportive places where kids could play, learn and work. Survey results also echoed the sentiment of youth organizers that there was too much focus on punishment and not enough on supporting youth.

In addition to conducting the survey, youth researched the Oakland budget, visited youth-serving facilities and presented their findings to local organizations and policymakers. All their research con-firmed what the young people observed in the surveys reported: there weren't enough resources for kids and what resources did exist were underfunded and understaffed.

During this same time period, staff and youth members of the Narcotics Education League's Centro de Juventud (who were also work-ing with PUEBLO on the surveys) attended a workshop on youth devel-opment at the University of California at Berkeley. The workshop provided important insights on how to craft programs that focused on developing young people's strengths and building youth leadership and power. The group was interested in bringing youth development approaches to bear on the issues raised by the survey and wanted to dis-cuss possible strategies for moving ahead.

Centro's Rosalinda Palacios, EBACY's Dave Kabashiya and PUEBLO's Danny HoSang met to discuss how they might advance an agenda that would result in long-term funding and support for youth development. San Francisco had passed Proposition J four years before, which provided a funding stream for youth programs in the city. The group wanted to explore the potential for success for such an initiative in Oakland. They mulled over whether to take the issue directly to the city council or to make it a ballot initiative.

Palacios recalled, "That's when we started thinking, 'We don't want to ask the city council for another penny because it's going to be a battle; always begging for money—for kids! So we decided, no, we're going to let the voters decide."[17]

The city council and other agencies were also looking into ways to respond to the youth's findings. City council member Sheila Jordan had convened a youth advisory group to make their own report to the city council. Urban Strategies Council (a nonprofit research and policy organization working on youth issues) was developing a comprehensive plan of its own. Palacios and others committed to youth development and activism wanted to get beyond plans and proposals originating from one entity that would build capacity and resources for only one or two groups. As she recounted:

> Nobody was thinking, "Well, wait a minute, why don't we get monies to spread it out evenly across the city and everyone work on advancing the concept of *youth development*." We need to change the paradigm. We don't need city hall telling us what to do. We need the community telling city hall what we think is best for kids.[18]

For Palacios, HoSang and Kabashiya, this paradigm shift would take the form of a ballot initiative that actually shifted the money to residents and built in more community input and control over how it was used. In 1995, the three organizations convened a meeting with key allies, including Millie Cleveland from the West Oakland Mental Health Center, youth and adult members of Youth Alive, and Paul Brekke-Meisner, who was with Oakland Public Schools. They invited Margaret Broadkin of San Francisco's Coleman Youth Advocates to talk about that group's successful effort to get Proposition J passed. The meeting focused on examining the feasibility of passing a similar initiative in Oakland.

Qualifying for a ballot initiative would require collecting a minimum of 30,000 signatures (or 15 percent of the city's registered voters). This small core group of nonprofit organizations needed to figure out if they could pull it off. HoSang, a seasoned organizer and trainer, helped the group conduct a strategic assessment of the political terrain as well as identify how they might get the necessary financial and human resources.

Each of the core partners brought important strengths to the coalition. PUEBLO's staff and membership had engaged in community organizing in Oakland for years over a broad range of issues and had a number of successful campaigns to its credit. EBAYC and Centro leadership had a history of combining direct services, advocacy and neighborhood organizing in Asian and Latino communities, respectively. All of the partners had a history of participating in and seeking out multiracial, multi-ethnic coalitions. And after years of grassroots campaigns on issues ranging from the overconcentration of alcohol outlets in poor communities to bilingual education, they had a great deal of comfort in the policy arena.

Perhaps most important, the groups' decision to collaborate was their own. It wasn't mandated as part of any grant. They came together because they wanted to, they liked working together and they wanted to do something concrete that would make a real difference. At the heart of their collaboration were shared values, mutual respect and the fact that each group came to the table with power—and a contribution to make. They decided to call their campaign Kids First!

GATHERING SIGNATURES AND SUPPORT

Much of the campaign's resources came from in-kind donations from individuals and community groups and a base of more than 200 volunteers (most of them youth and young adults). The group also relied on pro bono legal help in crafting the initiative's language as well as volunteer help from a high-level political consulting firm in shaping the campaign strategy. Still, the group decided that they needed to hire a campaign manager if they were to meet the June, 1996 deadline for qualifying for the November ballot. Amos White, a young community organizer with extensive electoral experience, agreed to do the job.

In addition, the campaign decided to pay a limited number of professional petition gatherers to augment the volunteer activity. It's important to note that members of grassroots organizations, faith institutions, and parents and youth comprised most of the volunteer base. Though they stood to gain from the initiative's passing, youth-serving organizations and youth advocacy groups did not choose to participate much. In any case, White was the only dedicated campaign staff and according to Palacios, "The effort nearly killed him but having him was really key." [19]

From March through June 1996, the Kids First! Campaign combed Oakland's neighborhoods to reach voters at supermarkets, bus stops, commuter trains and community events. Campaign workers wore bright purple T-shirts with the Kids First! name and logo emblazoned in day-glo orange. This uniform contributed to increasing public recognition and awareness. In fact, residents would spot the T-shirts and often stop the mainly young volunteers to ask how they could help support the measure.

White recalled one of the many examples of such community support. An older woman, who had passed him on his way to several church presentations, pointed to his T-shirt with excitement:

> She said, "You guys! I saw you!" And I'm standing there thinking, "Oh, God, what did one of my volunteers do?" And she said, "You're everywhere! I'm going to vote for that." And then she stops as I go walking by and she says, "What does it mean again?" She didn't know but she knew that T-shirt. She saw that T-shirt. That T-shirt had kids underneath it all over town; kids under the age of 18 who were registering people to petition. And yes it is legal. We had parents or adults there overseeing them. But that's how we had it. I had 500 of those T-shirts and we literally had none left. [20]

Early, positive media exposure also helped jump-start the initiative. Since there was no organized opposition, the real challenge was mobilizing the necessary resources among the coalition (which had now expanded to more than 40 organizations and hundreds of individuals) to collect their goal of 50,000 signatures over the remaining three months (to ensure that at least 30,000 were valid). That was about 16,700 per month, 554 per day, and 56 signatures per hour working 10 hours a day, seven days a week. It was tough work and the coalition had figured out they probably wouldn't meet the June deadline. The campaign decided to take the bold move of turning in the signatures two weeks after the deadline and daring the city to disqualify the measure. [21]

As planned, the coalition turned in 50,000 signatures to the city clerk two weeks after the deadline amid a spirited rally and press event attended by more than 100 people—many of them youth. The city accepted the petition for the November ballot and in August, 1996 validated that Kids First! had well over the 30,000 signatures required to qualify. With a little lobbying and pressure, the coalition passed the final step—city council approval—and the initiative was officially placed on the ballot as Measure K (for Kids First!). [22]

The initiative would create a charter amendment to set aside 2.5 percent of Oakland's General Fund exclusively for youth development and services to children and youth under 21 years old. The set-aside was to augment existing funding; the initiative prohibited reducing the total support for young people below the current (1995–96) fiscal year level. The initiative also established a 19-member Planning and Oversight Committee (POC), of which at least nine members must be under 23. The committee would make decisions as to how the money would be distributed.

TAKING IT TO THE POLLS AND BEYOND

During the election phase of the effort, campaign members worked to educate organizations about the initiative. Labor unions were particularly key as Kids First! campaign members met with the Police Officers' Association, the local teacher's union and the Service Employees International Union (which represents most city employees) to explain how the initiative worked and its impact on the public funding process. It was important to the coalition that public employees did not see Measure K as a threat to other public monies that paid their salaries.

The campaign also sought to expand the grassroots support it had gained during the signature-gathering phase by contacting voters frequently through precinct walks, phoning, community events and information tables at faith institutions, community centers and in high-traffic areas. Campaign headquarters also sent out weekly alerts by fax to organizations and the media (including neighborhood and organizational newsletters) and contacted thousands of people in businesses, nonprofits, schools and churches for endorsements, volunteers and money. The campaign could only afford one direct-mail piece, which it mailed right before the election. Phones were made available by some nonprofit groups but there weren't always enough phones to go around, so most of the voter outreach was conducted face-to-face.

Money was always an issue for the campaign, which hustled and scraped together resources as best it could. Its first major fundraiser came in October—less than a month before the election. Local artists and businesses donated items for an auction that raised thousands of dollars for the campaign. It was this money that bought the mail piece, window signs and kept the small staff going through election day.

When the votes were counted on November 5, 1996, Measure K had garnered the support of more than 75 percent of Oakland voters. Youth played a central role in the victory. They provided both volunteer support and leadership for this campaign to get funding to address the issues they had articulated two years before. The fact that there was no opposition didn't hurt either. Still, it was an amazing effort to pull off such a large undertaking with so few resources. The core group's commitment to moving ahead with the initiative without much money in hand had been risky. But it was key to taking the concrete steps that brought Measure K from idea to reality.

Right after the election, the core group got together to discuss next steps. According to Palacios:

> We said, "O.K. Do we disband now or do we stick together? If we stick together, what do we stick together around? If we disband, we just let the POC [Planning Oversight Committee] develop its own course." We basically said, "We're the parents of this initiative. We have to continue to be involved," so we made a political decision to continue as a collaborative.[23]

Two days after the election, the core group announced the formation of the Kids First! Coalition (KF!C) to oversee the POC process, ensure that grassroots adults and youth got appointed to the POC, and see that the city adhered to the terms of the initiative. The coalition had its work cut out for it, as youth advocacy organizations that had contributed little to the campaign now began pushing for their own agenda without resident input or support—a total contradiction of the original group's commitment to community control. Further, the city resisted disclosing the amount of money in its general fund and even attempted to restrict large amounts of money so that youth programs got a significantly smaller cut than the initiative's 2.5 percent set-aside initially projected. At this writing, the group was considering legal action to force compliance.[24]

Like most initiatives involving money, the process of carrying out policy based on the initiative became mired in political jockeying and was more complex than envisioned. In retrospect, many coalition members wished they had known more about the city's budget when they crafted the initiative and that they had opted for an entity besides the city to administer the fund. The measure did prescribe how the fund should be operated and set limits on administration costs at five percent and on evaluation costs at three percent, but without cooperation from the city, it was hard to monitor actual dollar amounts.

Perhaps the hardest part was ensuring that youth development remained at the center of programs funded through the measure. The group found early on in the implementation process that few organizations had a clue about what youth development actually was and wanted the money to do the "same old tired, top-down programs." Developing venues for training and capacity building among local agencies would be key in making youth development the primary model among service providers.

Yet, there were early positive outcomes. Youth involvement and leadership began to change the funding process. Youth members of the POC fought for more youth-led approaches, including setting aside money for youth-to-youth grants and job development. The young people participating in the POC received months of training and preparation from independent consultants for their role on the committee. Most were organizers who had some involvement in the initiative and that experience plus training made a difference. Youth are much more knowledgeable and confident in their new role as policymakers and they are effective advocates.

As the implementation process continues to unfold, it's clear to coalition members that the fight is far from over. Said Palacios, "We didn't want to establish a bureaucracy. We want the money to go to the community. KF!C is in it for the long haul to make sure that's exactly what happens."[25]

Final Thoughts

This chapter has described several initiatives designed to address pocketbook issues for families or organizations. Living wage and numerous environmental justice initiatives focus on how the lack of public accountability has resulted in poverty wages and unhealthy environments. The Kids First! Initiative focused on creating funding for youth-serving organizations by forcing the city to set aside a portion of its budget as a public investment in the community's young people. All are examples of creative ways of developing practical, institutional handles for addressing broad issues of government accountability.

There are plenty of other, similar policies designed to address institutional accountability. New Jersey has laws that punish corporate downsizing. Connecticut requires that companies receiving subsidies must stay in the state for ten years or pay them back. Minnesota's Corporate Welfare Reform Law requires that a business that receives state or local economic assistance must create a net increase of jobs in Minnesota within two years or pay back the aid. The granting agency establishes wage-level and job-creation goals.

In each case, communities want more from the public and private institutions that make the economy go. They want standards that include respect for the environment, a living wage, community stability and commitment to community development. In short, communities are less apt to fall for the old story that regulation will end up killing jobs and hurting business. These initiatives are proving just the opposite. The key is presenting the right kind of information that helps the public to understand and support the positive effects of regulation. Too often, advocates expect policymakers and community members to support initiatives because "it's the right thing to do" without taking into account economic concerns. The campaigns in this chapter prepared for industry's anti-regulatory arguments and worked to shift the terms of debate to focus on the needs of people—not purely on profit.

The most successful community campaigners don't get caught up in the policy process; instead, they use the policy process to advance their long-term organizing goals. With nearly 30 years' experience, it's no wonder that ACORN has a jump ahead of most groups in this area. However, living-wage, right-to-know (laws that force company disclosure of toxics) and other local policy campaigns are creating new partnerships and new "veterans" with impressive victories under their belts.

The role of community organizers is critical to these campaigns. Community organizing encompasses a discrete set of skills and knowledge that is particularly appropriate for the promulgation of policy work. All of the campaigns highlighted in this book were run by people with community organizing experience and sensibilities. Yet, organizations and funders often mistakenly look for staff with other professional backgrounds to run policy initiatives. Many of the federally funded prevention initiatives hire staff with graduate degrees in public health or trained in one of the health professions and then wonder why they have not been able to make significant inroads in community and policy development. It would be more effective for these initiatives to hire people with community organizing backgrounds (and develop advisory panels of content experts); it would also be useful for initiative staff who are not community organizers to have more opportunities to learn community organizing techniques. That way, they would be better prepared for the complicated work of creating policy change.

There are so many models and precedents that have been set in just the last few years that organizations seeking to mount a public or corporate accountability campaign don't have far to look for ideas. Policy development is a process, so the models are constantly changing. What wasn't possible last year might not be considered extreme enough next year.

Clearly, these initiatives have tapped into deep public concern about quality of life issues and this concern is pushing groups to try new, more comprehensive policies.

The best policy seeks to be innovative: it breaks the box but doesn't reinvent the wheel. Public health groups, in particular, would do well to explore how tools like living-wage campaigns and budget set-aside initiatives can move advocates beyond lamenting the connection between poverty and poor health status to doing something about it.

4

PLOTTING A COURSE:

Lessons from the Front Lines

Our nettlesome task is to discover how to organize our strength
into compelling power.

—DR. MARTIN LUTHER KING, JR. [1]

Each of the efforts described in the case studies in the previous two chapters combined grassroots organizing, media savvy and mastery of the policy process (often with the aid of pro bono lawyers) to get policy initiatives enacted. This chapter explores the process of developing a policy initiative from conceptualization to enforcement, along with common pitfalls and tools for effective advocacy.

The basic underlying principles for developing a policy initiative are, in the main, community organizing principles. At its heart, community-based public policy work is compelling powerful "others" to act in communities' interests—which is essentially effective organizing. Like a good policy initiative, a good organizing plan builds support, neutralizes opposition, and competently engages the media. The Midwest Academy provides excellent resources on the art and science of this kind of organizing, including their especially good guide, *Organizing for Social Change: A Manual for Activists in the 1990s* by Bobo, Kendall and Max (see page 169). Much of the organizing approach explored in this chapter is heavily influenced by their work.

Policy work is also more than organizing and making demands and those nuances are explored here as well. There are organizers who shy away from policy work because it can take years to achieve results—a definite "no-no" for those looking for the short-term win. There are policy people who shy away from organizing because they don't like the accountability or the "hassle" of having to check in with constituents as they wheel and deal with policymakers. Both are striving for a certain kind of expediency that doesn't serve communities well in the long term.

Effective policy work requires long-term tenacity and a strict attention to often arcane details in both the policy process and the organizing process. Both processes—and their points of intersection—are dealt with below.

Defining an Issue

An issue is defined as a broad problem area, like unemployment, youth violence, or teen pregnancy. There are always lots of issues to choose from. Recent incidents may make a particular issue "hot" for a community, as when youth violence leads a community to advocate for control on young people's access to handguns.

Some of the best policies address a community's vision of what it would like to become instead of focusing on community problems or deficits. Usually, when a community works from a place of vision, they manage to address a number of problems, too. One example is found in the growing number of local policies to increase the amount of a community's green space (protected natural areas for recreation and rest). Although these policies are a result of the residents' vision of their community as a beautiful place to live, increasing the number of parks in the community also helps to address issues of blight, youth development and negative land uses.

Sociologist John McKnight and his colleagues at Northwestern University pioneered a method of community mapping that enables neighborhoods to chart their assets and develop strategies for addressing issues based on their strengths. Used primarily in public health and community development efforts, asset mapping is a valuable tool for any group seeking to organize around any issue. The process includes conducting detailed surveys of institutions and individuals and building networks that help leverage both individual and institutional assets. You can learn more about this process in *Building Communities from the Inside Out: A Path Toward Finding and Mobilizing a Community's Assets*, by Kretzman and McKnight, which includes a number of case studies and project ideas for implementing such a process. This book, among other resources, can be helpful in structuring a more positive approach to policy development (see page 169).

The best way to choose an issue is to judge it against a set of criteria developed by group consensus that takes into account group and/or community values and interests—that is, what's important. Common criteria for a good issue include:

- It will make a positive difference in our community
- It's local, immediate and specific
- We can win
- It's clear and easy to understand
- It has a clear target
- It can help us raise money, volunteers and/or other resources
- It's consistent with our overall vision and goals
- After working on this, we'll be in a better position for the next campaign

Some veteran organizers have distilled these criteria into what they call the WRIST test. For every initiative they consider, they ask is it:

- **W**innable?
- **R**eal?
- **I**mmediate?
- **S**pecific?
- **T**angible?

According to Baltimore Citywide Liquor Coalition organizer Kevin Jordan, issue development is one of the most important steps in developing a policy advocacy strategy. It will determine your allies, your target and your power base. In fact, organizers who use the WRIST criteria have a saying that illustrates its importance: "If you want to make a fist, you've got to have a WRIST."

IDEAL INTERESTS AND REAL INTERESTS

Community values and interests are the ideal visions and the down-to-earth concerns we carry in our daily lives. They range from dreams of a safe, green world for all families to live in to fears that the "wrong kind" of neighbors will move in. Advocates must factor in community sentiment from both ends of the spectrum in order to identify issues that will have meaning for all the people with whom we work.

As organizer Greg Akili often says, interests are usually divided into two categories: ideal interests and real interests. Ideal interests are usually articulated in lofty vision statements such as, "a great future for all children." Real interests are those issues with a clear, concrete impact on our daily lives, such as the company bottom line, our property values, the quality of our children's schooling, the dangers of our jobs. Advocates often focus on ideal interests and pay little attention to real interests when choosing issues and framing their initiatives. How often do progressive groups justify their issue by saying, "It's the right thing to do"? How often does the opposition say, "It costs money and jobs"? A good issue provides your group with opportunities to encourage community visioning and hope but is grounded in the real interests and concerns of people "where they are."

For example, when Chicago activists were developing an ordinance to regulate alcohol and tobacco billboards, they discovered that many of the city's billboards were put up without permits. Not only were these billboards illegally placed, their owners had not paid the requisite permit fees. The group could have framed their proposed billboard initiative any number of ways. They could have focused on "ideal investments," such as protecting young people from the advertising. Instead they made the central issue the loss in revenues from illegal billboards and the need to develop more stringent regulations and enforcement. City officials certainly paid attention to the revenue argument, while community groups advanced an initiative they believed would make their neighborhoods a better place to live.

Organizational considerations in developing criteria

All advocacy must operate within the framework of your organization's purpose and long-range goals. Is this the appropriate issue for your group? It's important to compare your organization's goals with the goal for your issue. In your assessment you should ask yourself: What constitutes victory? How will this effort address the problem/have an impact on the quality of life of our clients/members and/or community? How will working on this issue advance our organizational goals to build more leadership, fight racism and injustice, or address other goals?

Another important consideration is your organizational health and survival. Can you win? Or perhaps more important, can your organization afford to lose? If done well, advocacy campaigns can strengthen organizations by building a sense of team spirit, expanding the leadership base, deepening the leadership's level of experience and expanding an organization's membership and contact base. If done poorly, the same campaign can drain an organization's human and financial resources. Of course, your organization must bring something to the campaign in the first place (i.e., membership, staff, money, reputation, facilities, press contacts, allies, etc.). Make a careful assessment of your assets as well as any liabilities you bring to the effort.

EFFECTIVELY "CUTTING" THE ISSUE

How you present an issue can make a difference in whether it appeals to the public and policymakers and gets taken up as a cause to be acted on. Campaigns to stop Uptown cigarettes in Philadelphia (see page 133) and X brand cigarettes in Boston (see page 130) were each developed around two points: the exploitation of important cultural values and institutions to sell deadly products, and these products' potential appeal to youth. In each case, it was clear to advocates that African Americans were being targeted by these companies, but targeted marketing was not enough of a "hook" to draw broad support. By "cutting" the issue in ways that emphasized its racial overtones and placing it within a context of ongoing efforts for socio-economic justice, advocates were able to broaden its appeal—and newsworthiness.

For example, in the X brand Campaign, activists felt that the cigarette manufacturer was attempting to use the association with the name of late human rights activist Malcolm X to sell cigarettes. Further, the large "X" on the package and its red, black and green colors seemed meant to target African American youth. Activists framed X brand as the latest in a long line of attacks against African Americans. They ran an emotion-charged campaign that compared the brand's name and marketing tactics to slavery, the infamous Tuskeegee Experiments (where African-American men with syphilis were left untreated in order to observe the disease in its last stages), and other forms of oppression.

Another example of adept "issue cutting" is found in the Baltimore Citywide Liquor Coalition's efforts to ban alcohol and tobacco billboards in most areas of Baltimore. Here again, themes emphasizing that the billboards targeted youth and exploited issues of race and class proved effective in mobilizing communities—with a local twist. The Coalition successfully transcended apathy around tobacco control by linking billboards to "bread-and-butter" issues of neighborhood blight, racial bias and needed economic development.

The Role of Information and Research

Policy initiatives should have a strong foundation in research that supports the initiative's specific strategy or approach toward addressing the problem. This is of particular importance in the case of progressive regulatory policies, as they usually receive greater scrutiny than policies perceived to be pro business. The extra scrutiny can be a good thing, as it forces proponents to make sure their policies will have an effect on real-life issues that are of concern to communities.

Initiatives should start with a strong and respectable data base of relevant information. Groups don't have to start from scratch or conduct their own studies. There are an incredible number of studies that have never been widely disseminated that can support progressive initiatives. In children and family services, for example, there are literally hundreds of well-crafted studies that examine the impact of poverty on children, and hundreds more on drug policy, employment, race relations and so forth. A search of the various social science indexes or a guided surf on the Internet can be very helpful in this regard.

Data can guide the development of an initiative in at least two ways. First, they can indicate the impact and severity of the problem and justify social action. Second, by showing that some groups are disproportionately affected by a problem, the data establish that the problem is linked to specific social and environmental factors, thus directing how the policy should be targeted.

Practically speaking, research should provide a clear analysis of the issues your group wants to address. It is one thing to say, "We have a problem with youth drinking." It's quite another to say, "We have alcohol-related problems because merchants are selling alcohol to local youth at these particular stores." The difference is community-based research. Gather as many reports, surveys, personal observations and other resources as you can that accurately describe the problem in order to identify effective policy options. Using the youth drinking example, it would be helpful to know, among other things, the number of arrests, injuries and other incidents related to youths and alcohol, where alcohol is purchased by young drinkers, what kind and brand of alcohol youth prefer, and where they go to consume it.

Research can shed light on existing policy initiatives and suggest new ones. When community groups in Oakland, California formed a coalition to fight youth access to alcohol and tobacco, they expected to propose policy initiatives to regulate billboard advertising of these products. However, research conducted on possible policy options and their effectiveness in other communities indicated that their efforts might be better rewarded if they focused on issues of licensing alcohol outlets. The group adjusted their strategies accordingly and moved on their city council soon after. In less than a year, they had convinced their council to pass what is currently among the strongest ordinances regulating alcohol outlets in California—one that included the passage of a moratorium on new outlets in certain high-density areas.

Another reason to have detailed information to substantiate policy recommendations is that all legislation must be based on findings or a set of facts that provide the rationale for enacting the law. These findings are important because they constitute much of the legal case if the law is challenged in court. Above all, the information should clearly describe the problem in ways that help your community, coalition, and the media grasp how serious it is.

Research and information-gathering should start in the *beginning* stages of developing an initiative. Most of this research cannot be confined to the library. Activists often identify these issues by spending time talking with their neighbors, walking around observing their neighborhoods with "fresh eyes," and identifying both the assets (or protective factors) and factors that put neighbors at risk.

ENVIRONMENTAL FACTORS

Identifying risk and protective factors requires attention to a community's environment, or the *context* in which these assets and challenges exist. Any behavior or activity operates within a context that shapes it. Assessing environmental factors in a community means shifting the focus from individual problems to the context in which these problems take place. This shift is important because environmental factors can play a major role in proliferation and *prevention* of problems in a community. This shift from an individual to an environmental perspective is much like widening a camera lens angle from a simple portrait to capture the "big picture" or landscape that surrounds it. There are different levels and dimensions of a community landscape.

Risk factors are those policies, issues, norms, problems, needs, deficiencies, etc., that are barriers to healthy communities. Protective factors are those norms, institutions, policies, etc., that support and enhance community health and development. All communities have both. Some factors will fit under both categories.

Physical or land-use factors. Buildings, roads, open space, institutions, businesses or lack of them are all a part of the physical infrastructure that form the foundation of a community.

Availability of goods and services. What we eat, wear and read is largely determined by what's available to us. The category of goods and services encompasses more than simply what we can buy: it also includes public services like schools, hospitals, water and recreational facilities. When looking at goods and services, it is important also to assess how accessible these services are to residents. For example, if a nearby recreation center has no wheelchair ramp or offers no classes in Spanish, it may not be useful to neighbors who cannot use the services without them.

Institutional factors. What is the impact of institutional behavior on the community? Public agencies can treat residents like constituents and stakeholders or like the "mob at the gates." Are companies good citizens? Do they hire local residents and invest in the community? Or do they take big tax breaks and subsidies and pollute the local environment? Public institutions such as social service organizations and government agencies can be accessible or hostile by limiting office hours, refusing to provide services or developing excessively complex access policies. It's important to understand the impact of private and public institutions on the community.

Human factors. Who lives here? What organizations do they belong to? Is there a history of concern for community well-being? What health indicators are there? What is the quality of family life? These are "portrait" questions that help to paint a clearer picture of who you are working with. Human factors explain what is going on for community members, the other factors help to explain why.

LISTENING TO THE COMMUNITY

Identifying risk and protective factors is important, but equally critical is knowing which factors are most crucial to address. Beyond collecting data and conducting research, an equally important way to gather information is to listen to people in the community: this can help you identify the dreams and ideas that inspire people—and the language they use to describe them. Chapter 1 discussed the "hidden transcript," the conversations that people without much power have about social change. Methodic listening can help surface this transcript and help you frame your initiatives more effectively. Pay attention to recurring phrases and themes and apply them to media messages as you develop them. Every coalition should have systems for collecting community input and feedback.

Here are a few examples of community-focused methods of "listening":

Surveys. Whether by phone, online or at the door, surveys are structured ways of getting community input and identifying issues and the prevalence of problems or attitudes. One should take care not to develop long, complicated survey instruments, ones that focus only on a community's problems. When done well, surveys enable groups to collect standardized data on a wide variety of issues and, through contact, encourage resident participation in the policy process.

Canvassing. Going door-to-door unannounced can be a good way to reach new people who aren't on anyone's list, raise public awareness, and build name recognition in a neighborhood. However, it is difficult to carry on an extensive conversation, for the most part, so input gathered will be limited.

Focus groups. One can gather solid, qualitative input from a small group—especially a group whose members have something in common or are in some way demographically similar. Just listening to the exchange between participants can be very enlightening and reveal more about the interests and concerns in a community than a two-way survey. The kind of information collected at focus groups can form the basis for subsequently gathering quantifiable data.

One-on-one interviews with key players. Listening is one of the most important tools for building relationships. Listen actively, with your whole body facing the speaker. Ask questions and probe deeper. Mostly, after offering a guiding question or two, just follow where the conversation leads you. Suspend your expectations and your agenda for the time being. Just listen to learn more about the other person and their concerns. Take notes if you need to and if it's not too obtrusive.

Walkabout. Identify a route in an affected or representative neighborhood. The route should provide a mix of things to observe (businesses, institutions, etc.) and take no more than 60 minutes to walk. If much of the business district is abandoned, that's worth observing, too. It's best to conduct this method in a small group. Encourage participants to take notes and to pay attention to both assets and challenges and debrief the group's observations upon return.

Defining a Policy Goal

The policy goal should be easily understood and should meet as much of a group's criteria as possible. A good goal requires cutting or shaping the issue into effective, doable action that engages community interest and support. When developing policy initiatives, try to incorporate features that help to address your coalition's long-term vision. A good policy can:

Build community capacity. Effective policy helps improve conditions in the community and creates more involved community members. The experience of advocating for the policy, when done well, expands the base of leadership.

Pay for itself. Advocates must develop creative ways to fund new policies. One way is user fees, where the licensee or the store owner—or whoever is using the service or selling the product—must pay a fee for the privilege of using that service or selling that product. Examples: local permit fees for alcohol and/or tobacco outlets, or conditional use permit fees for certain environmental land uses such as billboards, gas stations, or auto repair shops. A handy formula for calculating fees is to divide the cost of regulating the activity or enforcement by the number of projected "users."

Another way is to require that funds be diverted, such as through public funding set-asides, special levies or other means, to support policy implementation. Some organizations include economic development plans within their policy initiatives with an eye toward self-sufficiency in the long term. For example, an ordinance to develop affordable housing could include a plan for commercial development to subsidize project costs.

Solve real problems. When developing a policy, ask yourself: How does this solve the problem? Your answer should be clear, concise and to the point. Can you sum up the policy's impact in 25 words or less? If not, it's not clear enough.

Contribute to a sense of community. How do we regulate land use? Through closed administrative hearings for developers or at open community hearings administered by neighborhood people in their own neighborhood? Which is easier? But which will bring more people together, give them a sense of their own power and build a new cadre of skilled leadership?

What do we do to develop policies for seniors? Do we work to pass an initiative to fund programs? Or do we work to change policies at financial institutions to fund community development and affordable housing? Which one builds bureaucracy? Which one builds capacity?

Lay the foundation for more good policy. Look to the future. Each policy should be an incremental step on the path toward your larger goals. The policy you develop today should open the door, set the stage for further progress tomorrow. What will you gain from this initiative? How will it bring you closer to your ultimate goals?

Bring us closer to our ideal world. We have to reflect upon and revisit that ideal place, that place in our dreams where the world is the best possible place. We must make sure that whatever we do will, in the long run, help make that dream a reality.

Which Policy Approach to Use?

Before undertaking any initiative, it is important to ascertain which policy approach is best to address the issue at hand. Policy isn't always legislation. Sometimes it just isn't practical to get legislation enacted. It may be too soon to try to address the problem that directly, so other actions are needed to set the groundwork for regulation down the line. Advocates have a number of tools they can choose from that can be used instead of legislation—or as a complement to legislative strategies. The four most common policy actions (in addition to legislation) are voluntary agreements, lawsuits, moratoriums and mandated studies.

VOLUNTARY AGREEMENTS

Voluntary agreements are pacts between a community and one or more institutions that outline conditions, expectations, or obligations without the force of law. This is a good option to use when there isn't enough support to enact more formal regulations. Voluntary agreements need not be limited to cordial words and a handshake. Communities can still negotiate written memoranda of understanding that clearly spell out the conditions of the agreement.

Getting a solid agreement still requires research and organizing. It helps to start by identifying all of the institutional actors that have an impact on the issue. Once these actors are identified, research their role in creating the problem along with possible actions they could take to reduce harm in the community. Then, develop a "wish list" of actions you'd like the institution(s) to undertake. Since this agreement will not have the force of law, it's especially important to identify both "sticks" and "carrots" for institutional participation as well as any community power to back up an agreement. For example, think about the consequences for violating the agreement. What, if any, would be rewards for compliance? You can impose fines, or revoke relevant licenses or permits. Tax rebates or public subsidies could be tied to institutional compliance as well.

Of course, it will take some negotiating and community pressure to actually reach an agreement. Make sure no one from your community group ever negotiates alone. At least two members of your coalition should be present at all times.

LAWSUITS AND OTHER COMPLAINTS

Lawsuits and other court actions can be both tedious and expensive. Therefore, groups should carefully consider all options before deciding to take on a lawsuit. If an organization has the resources (in staff, money or pro bono legal support), a well-framed legal intervention can accomplish much in both the short term and long term—even if it simply gets the other side to the table. The framing of any action is important. Care should be taken to name the right defendants, including parent companies and others who profit from the action that your group wants stopped.

One legal action that activists can learn much from is the skillful use of *interrogatories*—requests for information and documents from the opponents. In some cases, groups will consult with other activists to identify useful information for regulation beyond the current legal action. For example, one group engaged in a lawsuit against an alcohol company solicited items for their interrogatory from alcohol policy activists nationwide. The documents yielded from that single lawsuit provided the foundation for years of policymaking—even though the case was eventually settled out of court.

Other legal actions commonly pursued by groups include requesting injunctions against the implementation of laws before they have had a chance to take effect; organizing victims with standing (those with a stake in the issue) to sue polluters or other institutions causing damage to a community; and mounting civil suits when an institutional action has a pattern of discrimination or damage to certain populations (i.e., people of color, women, people with disabilities).

Sometimes, an organization has no choice but to get into the legal fray because it's hard to stand back and watch companies pollute or prey on consumers in violation of existing laws. Engaging in legal action in these cases is simply a matter of defending consumers legal rights. However, companies are increasingly suing local governments, groups and individual activists when they attempt to hold industries accountable. It is not uncommon for company attorneys to attend even the smallest public hearings in order to intimidate activists and public officials seeking to pass a regulation. Here are some examples:

- In Contra Costa County, California, a public hearing to decide the fate of eight alcohol and tobacco billboards brought as many as eight lawyers from the alcohol and tobacco industry.[2]
- After Oakland, California prevailed in a lawsuit partially funded by Anheuser-Busch to block the city's right to regulate local alcohol outlets, an attorney for Anheuser-Busch didn't mince words when he told the city council he would sue them "coming and going" if they passed a proposed billboard regulation.[3]
- A couple in Virginia who sought legal redress for extensive damages to their home and health from blasting by a nearby coal company were denied any compensation for these damages. The company sued the couple, claiming that their legal action caused the company to lose business.[4]

These lawsuits can be scary and distracting if not properly integrated into an organization's overall organizing strategy. The first and most important rule is never to keep a lawsuit or a company's threat of one a secret. Make sure to publicize the company's action widely. If the target of the lawsuit is the local jurisdiction that enacted the policy, your organization may be able to intervene with an attorney to ensure community interests are addressed. *Intervenor status* enables a community group to participate in a lawsuit and argue its case almost as if it were a defendant. This kind of participation can make a real difference when a local jurisdiction is not strongly committed to defending an ordinance in court.

In addition to initiating lawsuits, it also helps simply to file complaints about bad or illegal practices with the appropriate regulatory agencies. For example, alcohol ads that appeal to children violate laws in many states. Activities that cause pollution, unfair labor practices and obstructions to fair trade are other areas of regulation where violations can be challenged. If one regulatory agency is notoriously slow to act, try redefining the issue so it fits under the purview of a more active regulator. For example, redefining a violation from a bad business practice to a health concern often brings a whole new set of actors into play. Find out who enforces what relevant regulations and work accordingly.

MORATORIUMS

Sometimes you just need to stop policy activity until there can be further study of its impact and any possible alternatives. Common moratoriums include bans on new alcohol outlets, billboards, dump sites or office construction. It isn't enough to enact a time-limited ban; any moratorium policy should use the time to gather more information and assess future policy options.

MANDATED STUDY

Research can be costly and time consuming. If time and support allow, why not get local government to do the research? Through policy that mandates a study or data collection, public resources can be directed to do a thorough job of information gathering. The policy can set parameters for the kind of group or institution that can conduct the study, key questions framing the study, resident involvement and monitoring of the study, and the plan for dissemination and use of the results. A Los Angeles coalition got the city to conduct a study on wage levels. The resulting data were hard to dispute when it came time to discuss the need for a living-wage law. They were the city's own.

Identifying a Target

When developing an initiative goal, you must identify a target or decisionmaking body with the power to enact the changes sought. For example, should it be the city council through an ordinance? A company through its policy? A state through a new law? Each potential decisionmaking body or target will require different organizing strategies to move the target to action.

After the target is identified, extensive research must be done to identify each party's interests. You should find out, for example, what they care about, who provides them with support, and whether they have any personal relationship to your issue. Finding this out requires combing through public reports, contribution lists, news clippings and personal interviews to develop this information. Some advocates rely heavily on the Internet for this research. Using networks like the Institute for Global Communications' EcoNet, PeaceNet and LaborNet, advocates place queries online to gather intelligence and search for related documents.

A thorough analysis can lead a group to change to a more vulnerable target. Oftentimes, this shift is from a company that a group may have little power over to a regulatory agency where there is a higher degree of accountability. In the case of billboard regulation, for example, it was much easier to get state and local government to restrict the placement and content of billboards than to pressure the billboard industry to give up a significant portion of its revenue from alcohol and tobacco ads.

KEY QUESTIONS IN CHOOSING A TARGET

- Who or what institutions have the power to solve the problem and grant your demands?

- Who must you get to first before you can influence those with the real power?

- What are the strengths and weaknesses of each potential target? How are they vulnerable?

- Which targets are appointed? Elected?

- How do you have power or influence with them (as voters, consumers, taxpayers, investors, shaming, etc.)?

- What is their self-interest in this issue?

- Who would have jurisdiction if you redefined the issue (e.g., turned a tobacco advertising issue into a fair business practices issue)? Does this help you?

Don't confuse your target with the allies you need in order to win. Primary targets are always the individuals or decisionmaking bodies that ultimately have the power to grant the group's goals. There are lots of folk to work with and convince along the way, but they are not primary targets. Once the group has identified the goal and the target, they are ready to develop an action plan or a set of objectives and a timeline to make it happen.

ASSIGNING PRIMARY RESPONSIBILITY

The target and the goal of the initiative say everything about how your group is defining the problem—and who is responsible for solving it. Policies to regulate underage drinking that fine or arrest youth for possession focus on youth as the problem. Policies that fine or revoke the licenses of merchants who sell alcohol to youth focus on who profits from sales to minors. The key is to develop policies that balance institutional and individual accountability and go beyond education and punishment. The best policies address the social and economic context of the problem by shifting resources in ways that build greater agency and power at the community level.

Identifying Support

Rarely can one group get an initiative enacted working alone, so building broad support is critical to success. Oftentimes, building support requires building a coalition or group of organizations that come together temporarily for a specific reason. Coalitions are meant to be short term and are usually developed with a specific issue in mind. Every three to four months, there will be a need to rebuild a coalition or organization with a new group of people. People will either have moved on to another level, become involved in something else, or become inactive.

When assessing whether to put together a coalition, groups must identify what kind of support is needed to win, who is most likely to support the initiative, and who can influence the target.

To determine the amount of support needed to win, advocates usually start with how the target will make its decision. How many votes (if applicable) are needed to win? Once the votes are in, who will review and approve the decision? Who will make recommendations concerning the decision? After a careful review of the decisionmaking process (and any relevant deadlines), identify appropriate levels of support (i.e., minimum number of letters to be generated, attendance needed at public hearings, how many phone calls from constituents, etc.) for each step of the process.

Identifying likely supporters requires some knowledge of the community as well as an analysis of each potential partner's interests. It is important to start with a detailed and specific list of prospective allies. Do not, for example, automatically list the faith community as one ally because they are generally concerned about the community's welfare. Like other organizations, faith institutions are often overwhelmed with their own activities and will need to see your issue as high on their own list of priorities if they are to get involved. Identify specific groups and institutions and why they might get involved.

Likely supporters have both strong *self-interest* and deep *concern* about the issue your group is trying to address. They will also have *low risk* in joining you. Remember, often it is the big-name "leader-types" who have little self-interest and high risk (i.e., more to lose) in joining advocacy initiatives. Try to identify grassroots and other organizations with strong ties to the issue. Allies need not be formal organizations. For example, a group focused on passing a clean indoor air ordinance might first identify parents of children with asthma as primary allies—and not start building their coalition with popular ministers who have little attachment to the issue.

BUILDING A BASE

A good idea or a good issue will not get far if it only has the support of a few people. An organization must have a base of people that can be counted on to achieve its goals. Too often, not enough care is taken to develop a broad base of support for policy initiatives. In developing your base, consider what the benefits will be to those you want to join in the effort. Always ask yourself, "What am I offering?"

Veteran organizer Greg Akili talks about appreciating the total when recruiting support. He points out that too often, we complain because there are not more people involved. We miss critical levels of support because we only count the people who come to the regular meetings. Groups often have at least three levels of support: core supporters (usually about 5 to 7 people)—the key volunteers who can always be counted on; active supporters (usually 20 to 25 people)—folks who will support most of the activities and will attend some organizing meetings; and general supporters (usually 50 to 70 people)—people who will do one thing, one time and rarely come to organizing meetings.

The key is getting each level of support to move to the core by asking more from people at each level and showing appreciation for the core *and* for supporters at each "outer" level. Develop ways to assist people to move to a deeper level of involvement. Core supporters need to work with new people, conduct orientation and plan parties for new supporters. This is the essence of recruiting and retaining volunteers.

Recruiting volunteers is like working in a great sifter—the more you shake a sifter, the more its contents falls through the cracks. Building big numbers of volunteers requires talking to lots more people than you need—and making it very easy (not too many shakes!) for them to make a contribution. If it's too difficult to get involved (for example, if they have to call to find out where the meeting will take place, if there's no child care, if they have to make up a script to help you call volunteers, etc.) they will probably "fall through the cracks."[5]

SOME COMMON RECRUITMENT EQUATIONS

- In order to get 50 people to show up when the issue is not hot, 150 to 200 names are needed.

- If the names are "cold"—that is, people not familiar with the group or issue—more names will be needed.

- Thirty percent or more of the people called will not be at home; 15 to 20 percent of the telephone numbers will not be good numbers; 25 to 30 percent of the responses will be no; 25 to 30 percent of those reached will say yes. Of those who say yes, only a small percent will actually show.

- Using a "warm" list, out of 20 people talked to, nine will say yes and three to four will actually show.

When conducting recruitment efforts, keep in mind the following tips:

Recruit to action, not meetings. Everyone's time is precious. Make sure that you emphasize what your group will do when you get together, what you hope to accomplish and how each person can contribute.

Be sensitive to your personal presentation. Remember that when recruiting, appearances count! There are no hard and fast rules when it comes to presenting yourself but a little common sense can go a long way. For example, you would dress differently when making a presentation in an institution of faith than you would at an advocacy organization's picnic.

Be prepared; know who you are talking with. There's nothing more annoying to a potential volunteer than having someone call on them who knows little about their work in a community. Avoid the mistake that one zealous recruiter made: She spent an hour explaining to her potential recruit about the harms of tobacco and why it was an important issue in their community. She had no idea that the person with whom she was speaking was an expert in internal medicine who belonged to the national board of a cancer prevention organization. Knowing who you are talking with can help avoid these kinds of mistakes and give you ideas for "openings" that can make potential recruits more receptive to your approach.

COMMON METHODS FOR MOBILIZING VOLUNTEERS

HOUSE MEETINGS. These gatherings are often hosted by volunteers in order to organize a local area. The host will invite friends and neighbors to refreshments and a presentation on the issue by someone in coalition leadership.

PHONE BANK. Volunteers and/or staff call phone lists to recruit new volunteers.

CANVASSING. Staff and/or volunteers go door-to-door to raise public awareness of the initiative and recruit supporters.

There are certainly many more ways to get the word out but there's nothing like direct contact (either by phone or in person) to get people into action. It is important to develop recruitment systems, including scripts to prompt volunteers, and mechanisms for tracking, follow-up, rewards and accountability.

Establish your credibility. People get lots of requests for their time. It's important that you let them know a little about your skills and experience and what your group has accomplished. Organizing is mostly about building relationships. What experiences, friends, affiliations do you share that can help build a bridge between you? Getting involved can be risky—especially for someone with significant "standing" in a community. What credibility do you offer that can help allay any concerns?

Listen actively. Coalitions should reflect the common needs and interests of all participants, but how can you know what they are if you've never asked? When recruiting, probe and listen carefully for relevant self-interests, concerns, passions that motivate the person. When you listen at this stage, it sends the message that they will be "heard" throughout the process.

Challenge people to act in their interest. You've been listening and engaging with your potential recruit in a dialogue about their issues and concerns. *Now you must ask them if they are ready to do something about them.* A challenge need not be impolite. A simple, "Mrs. Smith, I see you are very concerned about the selling practices of the local convenience store. Our coalition could sure use your help in getting them to change. We have this ordinance we are trying to get passed that has really worked to control these kind of problems in other cities. We think it could work here. But we need your help…" Remember, try to match your request to the skills and availability of the recruit. Always have some specific volunteer options in mind—and not just going to meetings!

Get a commitment. Always ask the person directly for a commitment—and wait for the answer. "Yes" is great but a "no" is better than a "maybe" which more often means, "No, but I just don't want to tell you to your face," and wastes the recruiter's time in follow-up conversations. A common recruitment phrase is, "May I count on you to…?"

Follow up! Follow up! Follow up! Even when people make a commitment, they need to be reminded. Stay in touch with volunteers by providing them with updates, reminder calls (three for each meeting or action is typical), and lots of gratitude and recognition for every contribution they make. Having food at every meeting doesn't hurt either.

Power and Opposition

> If there is no struggle, there is no progress. Those who profess to
> favor freedom, and yet deprecate agitation, are men who want crops
> without plowing up the ground. They want rain without thunder and
> lightning. They want the ocean without the awful roar of its many
> waters. This struggle may be a moral one; or it may be a physical one;
> or it may be both moral and physical; but it must be a struggle.
> Power concedes nothing without a demand.
>
> —FREDERICK DOUGLASS [6]

Advocacy is controversial. After all, we wouldn't have to organize, plan and strategize if *everyone* agreed that our initiative was the perfect thing to do. Chances are, the initiative wouldn't have much of an impact if no one took issue with it. That is why savvy advocates understand and prepare for opposition. Of course, it's better not to have much opposition but it's far worse to be unprepared for what may arise.

Think strategically about your initiative. Are there interests that may be adversely affected? Will the initiative cost money? Raise fees or taxes? Increase regulation? Any of these can generate opposition. The best plan is to do your homework, understand in detail the impact of your initiative, and be ready to justify it to the decisionmakers you are targeting.

PLAN FOR OPPOSITION

A local coalition prided itself in its good relationships with virtually every decisionmaker in their small town. That was one reason they thought their initiative to get local police to track alcohol-related incidents using a simple form would go over unopposed. The group met with the local police chief in what started to be a friendly, comfortable meeting. The meeting soon turned difficult, leaving coalition members hurt and confused. How could they guess that their friend, the police chief, would get so upset about a little form that could do so much good?

The group had not researched procedures for the police department so they didn't know the amount of paperwork police were already responsible for. The coalition had to re-group and develop a new strategy: build widespread support for the data-gathering initiative in the community so it would be difficult to dismiss, while streamlining the process even further to address issues of police workload. Although there were coalition members who didn't go bowling with the chief as often as they used to, the initiative was eventually implemented.

What this coalition learned the hard way is that every initiative has an impact. Often, initiatives designed to improve public health adversely affect powerful interests. This can result in powerful opposition—and, sometimes, strained relationships. Reducing consumption of unhealthy products or limiting advertising of alcohol and tobacco are examples of common public health advocacy initiatives that affect industries' bottom line. Astute advocates remember that "real interests" are at stake and plan accordingly.

Usually, the target decisionmaking body is more receptive to the interests of industry than to those of local, community-based groups. Part of the reason is that industries employ lobbyists and government-relations staff who nurture relationships with officials as their full-time job. Another important reason is that, for elected officials especially, electoral campaigns require lots of money. Industry contributions are an important source of funds and officials are keenly aware of this fact.

Community groups still have power—even if they don't have money to throw around. They have people power, and enough of it will beat money power most every time. However, a coalition must be prepared to show its power if it is to get anything accomplished. In organizing, this is called *backing up your demand.*

WHY DEMAND AND NOT REQUEST?

Advocacy requires conviction and strength. Nevertheless, a demand need not be rude or inflexible. It is simply a statement of what your group wants and what it will settle for (usually called the *back-up demand*). Negotiation requires that the group focus on conditions, goals and impact—not on a rigid, pre-determined outcome. However, if your group has spent time researching the issue, listening to community concerns and developing an initiative based on constituent needs, then there is a responsibility to advocate for outcomes that are consistent with group values and consensus.

THE ACCOUNTABILITY SESSION

Holding an accountability session or meeting with your target (or a representative or portion of the target group) helps to make your demand clear and to assess the target's level of support. Ideally, the goal would be to get the target's commitment of support at the meeting.

Accountability sessions can range in tone and setting from a friendly, small meeting at the target's office to a large community hearing where the target is put on the spot. The setting and tone will be shaped by the group's history with the target and what kind of session best supports their overall strategy.

A community hearing as accountability session

A community hearing is a great way to focus attention on an issue, educate your neighbors and key local players, and have a public forum in which to hold your elected officials accountable. It takes hard work and effort to organize a community hearing, but one that is well attended can bring more than heightened awareness of the issue, it can also bring further recognition to your organization, identify additional volunteers and help strengthen local coalition-building efforts. You should consider doing a hearing if:

- You can get your elected official(s) to attend.
- You have a significant base of people who will come out to events if contacted.
- There is local interest in the issue(s) of concern.
- You can identify one or more people who are able to take the lead in organizing the hearing.
- You have or can acquire the resources to send notices, press releases and make follow-up calls.

If you cannot meet these conditions, then a hearing isn't really feasible. Spend your energies on strengthening the coalition instead.

IMPORTANT ISSUES TO CONSIDER WHEN PLANNING AN ACCOUNTABILITY SESSION

- Is the target hostile to the initiative?
- Does the target have a history of buckling under industry/opposition pressure?
- Does the coalition have trusted allies who could effectively reach the target?
- Will public pressure help or harm our efforts?
- What preparations must we make in order to have an effective session?
- What are the target's relevant interests/concerns?
- What are our demands? Back-up demands?
- Who's best to make the demand?
- What power do we have to back up our demands?
  (i.e., petitions, phone calls, letters, public shaming, recall, etc.)
- What are we willing to do? What are we not willing to do?

REMEMBER:

- Never make idle threats. Only warn about possible actions you are sure you can pull off. For example, don't tell a target that failure to support your initiative means losing the next election—unless you can back it up.

- Always represent the group ethically and professionally, regardless of how tough the session gets.

- Never send one person to meet with the target. Negotiations are tricky and always require at least one witness. Having others in the meeting also sends the message that this is a group action (not an individual one) and that those meeting with the target are accountable to the group for any outcomes of the session.

Preparing for the hearing. Identify a date that is relatively non-competitive with other important local events. It's hard to schedule an event that does not compete with anything. However, it is wise to make a few well-placed phone calls to make sure your tentative date works for key players.

Choose a location that many people already like to go to and are familiar with, has plenty of parking, is accessible to those with disabilities and can be reached by public transportation. Make sure to mention the bus or train lines that serve the location in all notices. Schools, churches or community service organizations are often ideal, inexpensive locations.

Put together an interesting panel to discuss and clarify the issue. Although you might want to include a researcher to add legitimacy to your position, make sure that person speaks in an accessible fashion. Think about what kind of panel would undermine the prevailing arguments against your initiative. For example, a line-up on regulating alcohol outlets might include a public health professional, a police representative, a local merchant concerned about overconcentration of liquor stores, a parent and a concerned minister or educator. You may have other resources to draw from.

Think about what kinds of people you would like to attend this hearing, such as neighborhood associations or parent groups. Invite groups that represent these kinds of people to help shape the hearings early on. They may have some great ideas of their own as well as providing needed help. You don't have to have a meeting to do this; the phone will do if you have a short timeline. However, a letter of invitation describing the issue and the plans for the hearing in detail can be very helpful—particularly for more formal organizations. At minimum, ask to use their name as an endorser or sponsor of the event and ask if they would be willing to share their mailing list.

Some helpful hints. Develop a notice that clearly states what the hearing is about as well as all the logistical information (i.e., time, date, place, directions by car or public transportation). If possible, include a listing of organizations supporting the hearing to lend increased credibility. If you will have refreshments (strongly recommended), say so on the notice.

Make sure you have a good mailing list(s) that contains local folk who are interested in this issue. You might want to contact organizations that have testified at any public hearings on this or a similar issue. As a rule of thumb, you'll need to send an announcement to at least four times as many names as the number of people you would like to attend.

In addition to doing a mailing, develop a speakers bureau to make presentations to local groups on the issue and invite them to the upcoming hearing. Work with your speakers to make sure they are clear on the issue and can translate it to others well. It may be important to identify speakers in languages beside English to address all significant populations in your community. Make sure to have translators at the hearing, if needed, and publicize the fact that translation will be available on notices in the appropriate language. Make sure to supply speakers with notices (translated if necessary), fact sheets and sign-up sheets so that you can follow up with a phone call later.

Keep track of people who commit to coming to the hearing and prepare to make reminder calls one to two days before the hearing.

Confirm site arrangements a week in advance. Make sure chairs, tables, microphones and public address system are all as you planned. Confirm how you will get into the site (do you need a key? will a maintenance person or community member be there to let you in?) and who to contact at that time if there is a problem. Clarify your obligations for clean up, closing, etc. Finally, make sure there is a follow-up plan for publicizing the results of the hearing after it has taken place.

Youth Organizing in Policy Efforts

Increasingly, community organizations are engaging young people in their policy initiatives. Some groups limit youth involvement to "photo opportunities" and "auxiliaries," where young people simply support adult-driven agendas. Other groups have developed youth-led initiatives, where young people identify policy initiatives and organize youth and adults to support them. The effort to enact Oakland's Measure K, for example (see Chapter 3), came about as a result of youth advocacy to defeat a curfew ordinance. Young people across the country are expressing growing weariness—and militancy—in response to policies that criminalize youth while cutting spending for youth services and programs. Further, as they organize to fight these anti-youth policies, young people are proving that there are other ways to affect the policy process besides voting.

The best youth advocacy incorporates elements essential to any organizing initiative (i.e., democracy and respect), while paying attention to the special requirements of youth work. The following is an exploration of some of these special requirements and examples of how groups have addressed them.

MAKING ROOM FOR YOUTH LEADERSHIP

Like anyone else, young people want a say in their organizations. Unfortunately, it is virtually impossible to engage youth in organizations led by and designed for adults. Adults can get impatient with youth input. Youth can get impatient with adult language and process. Even in the best youth-adult collaborations, young people need "safe space" to determine their own agenda and respond to their own needs, with the support of adults.

The Community Coalition for Substance Abuse Prevention and Treatment (CCSAPT) in Los Angeles is one of many organizing institutions working to build youth-led advocacy in their community. CCSAPT (see Chapter 2) is a grassroots organization dedicated to building residents' power in South Los Angeles, where changing demographics has meant an increasingly younger community. In order to truly organize the whole community, CCSAPT had to commit itself to building youth power as well.

At first, CCSAPT worked with youth by providing programs and events or by simply incorporating young people into their existing initiatives. For example, when the coalition focused on billboard regulation, youth counted billboards, provided testimony and participated in press events. Still, it was clear that there was a lot of untapped potential among the youth for leadership development.

CCSAPT's Solomon Rivera found that their organizing efforts really took off when they made room for young people to identify the issues that had meaning for them:

> Youth work is hard to pin down. At best, you're going to get youth involved for a couple of years and then they're going to be moving on to college or the work force....What's really helped [with CCSAPT] was [the youth] having their own distinct campaign around a local issue for them and getting away from some kind of "prevention type" program by being clear that we were trying to develop leaders, that this was going to be a politicized effort....There was going to be a lot of teaching about critical thinking and of certain political lines. There were youth who were attracted to that. Then there were the hot button issues.[7]

The hot-button issues were two initiatives on the 1994 California ballot. The first was the "three strikes" criminal justice initiative that would require life imprisonment for offenders convicted of a third felony. The second was the anti-immigration measure designed to strip immigrants of basic rights and legal protections. Given the ethnic composition of South Los Angeles, the two initiatives raised many emotional responses in the young people. Many of the advocates had been victims of police sweeps and believed that the criminal justice system was biased and arbitrary. For them, "three strikes" threatened to pull more young people of color into the penal system, where they were already unfairly overrepresented. Anti-immigration initiatives were also close to home, as their implementation would threaten the safety and livelihood of a number of youth participants and their families.

The youth worked hard to oppose these initiatives by canvassing, registering people to vote, and conducting voter registration and by organizing marches and rallies—both in concert with adults and with other youth organizations. Although both initiatives passed, the young people emerged from their efforts with a new sense of themselves as leaders. The three-strikes effort spurred them to think critically about the uses of public funding for criminalizing youth versus for education. Following the vote on the initiatives, Rivera and Marqueece Dawson worked with the youth to help them discuss and refine their concerns. It was out of this discussion that their first youth-led and youth-defined initiative to increase student input on school spending came about.

LEARN TO LET IT GO AND GROW

After three years of mentoring and leadership development, youth in CCSAPT now run their own high school site committee meetings. They develop their agendas, conduct the recruitment and work as an area-wide team to do their own strategic planning for the campaign. Rivera, Dawson and other CCSAPT staff still work closely with the youth but it is the young people who now drive the campaign. They are the ones conducting the research and doing the analysis while staff step back to more of a mentoring role. Says Rivera:

> Staff has played a primary role and will continue to for some time. We don't have them do a strategy chart from scratch. We kind of walk them through it and they recreate with us the power analysis that shapes our work. Certainly there is some level of understanding of the larger forces at work that staff have to bring to bear, but more and more youth are running their own meetings at the schools and at the Center. I'm constantly impressed with the amount of initiative they take....They come up with stuff that's often much better, much sharper than what the adults would've thought to do.[8]

YOUTH NEED SUPPORT FOR THEIR INVOLVEMENT

Working with youth requires tenacity and follow up that, more than adults, includes getting to know their families. Youth involvement often requires a great deal of support, including arranging for rides to meetings, food, and sometimes academic and family services. Colleen Floyd-Carroll organizes youth for a tobacco-prevention project housed at Contra Costa County, California's Community Wellness and Prevention Project. TIGHT (Tobacco Industry Gets Hammered by Teens) works through young adult and high school-aged organizers to mobilize kids of diverse backgrounds on tobacco control. Floyd-Carroll spends a significant amount of her time hooking kids up with support services, looking for jobs for their parents and in some cases, tracking kids in the juvenile justice system. She says,

> These kids are part of families. They are part of communities. If we are serious about wanting to involve all kinds of kids—poor kids, troubled kids as well as the student government 'leader' types—then we have to support their involvement with money, services, whatever they need. TIGHT provides salaries for organizers and stipends for high school coordinators.

Floyd-Carroll believes that providing resources has helped to diversify their organizing staff: "If you don't provide salaries, you only get the kids who can afford to work for free. [9]

LET YOUTH DO IT THEIR WAY

Taj James and the cadre of youth organizers at San Francisco's Youth Making A Change (Y-MAC) use a wide variety of tactics to engage young people in their organizing efforts. Poetry slams, open mikes for rap artists, graffiti art, house parties and documentary video are among the many activities they have devised to draw other young people into action. James and his colleagues also create space for political education, where young people read and discuss ideas, debate issues and simply express their views on a wide range of topics. There aren't a lot of places for political discussion and reflection, says James, where people can push themselves and try new things. The reading group has other added benefits, according to James:

> When you take the time to really reflect and sit back, when there's not a rally the next week or you're not, as a group, being pressed to move a specific agenda, [the study group] gives you a certain freedom to really push yourself and ask, "What is really going on?" And to analyze campaigns that we've been involved in collectively from different sides and say, "From our perspective this is what it looked like." [10]

The study group is comprised mostly of experienced youth organizers and a few older activists who act as mentors and griots—"historians" sharing lessons from the past. The group's multicultural composition has facilitated new working relationships in the area as young people develop ideas for collaborative, cross-cultural projects among the members. The multi-generational nature of the group has also yielded benefits. According to James, the older activists have been inspired by the youth to become more active and the youth benefit from the older members' wisdom and experience.

However, it has been the cultural work that has lured the most young people to Y-MAC. These more creative outlets have drawn the kind of young people who don't normally get involved in public policy work. Says James:

> There is a small number of young people who can be mobilized and are experienced, who will come out and attend hearings, but you're not going to get the vast majority....The youth started using cultural events as a way to get folks in, involved, and educated about the issues. [They] engage in sharing ideas and images and words as a way to build the general consciousness among young people.[11]

Y-MAC's efforts didn't stop at events. They were committed to bringing the creative energy of their cultural events directly into the policy arena. When Y-MAC joined the Justice for Aaron Williams campaign, an initiative to address police brutality in San Francisco, the group saw an opportunity to combine their cultural work with their policy efforts.

Aaron Williams was an African-American man who, in 1997, after being tied up, pepper sprayed and badly beaten by police, was left to die in the back of a police van without medical care. The issue was an emotional one in San Francisco, especially for young people who felt the police department had been particularly abusive in low-income communities. Youth reports of harassment by officers were all too common, according to Y-MAC members. They felt that what happened to Williams (although he was older) could have happened to any one of their members.

The officer who committed the beating and injury had a history of abuse and violations at the San Francisco Police Department and in his previous police work elsewhere—including the death of a developmentally disabled African-American man while under his custody. The campaign focused on getting policy enacted by the city's police commission that would place police under greater review and fire the officer involved.

Police commission meetings became the focal point of the organizing effort, as Y-MAC strove to make those hearings "people-oriented" meetings. Working with a larger coalition, they packed the hearings with hundreds of young people. The group also used the opportunity for public testimony as a venue for creative expression by the participants. In this way, they transformed the hearings from "strictly business," bureaucratic meetings to grassroots rallies and cultural events. James recalls:

> We started to have these mass meetings at the police commission and basically fought for control over the meetings. We were able to turn out folks in such numbers that we pretty much ran the meetings ourselves as sort of community meetings, as education sessions and rallies. One of the things we started at those meetings was having the young people share their culture. So when students went up to testify, they would read poems directed at the commissioners. That brought a lot of people to the microphone who wouldn't have spoken otherwise. It was really powerful to see how we were able to blend the cultural and the political in the same context.[12]

The coalition emerged victorious from that campaign with a larger cadre of young people who were politicized and ready for the next initiative—with cultural work playing a prominent role in their organizing. For the young people involved, this is one of the few activities that challenges them to bring their "whole selves" to their work. Most of all, it makes meaningful work fun.

LEARN ASPECTS OF YOUTH CULTURE

Dr. Thandi Hicks-Harper of Billo Communications, an organization dedicated to engaging youth in prevention activities, has conducted extensive focus group research with young people and youth-serving organizations. She has found that most organizations are clueless about youth language, music and other aspects of youth popular culture.

"The best initiatives effectively incorporate aspects of youth culture," she says. "They use youth's language and important cultural symbols. They have authentic and organic leadership of the effort." More and more, according to Hicks-Harper, that culture is grounded in hip hop. Hip hop music, dance, style of dress and visual arts have become the media of choice for a broad section of young people. Adult organizers who dismiss hip hop as all negative and "noise" run the risk of losing kids. "It's a matter of respect," says Hicks-Harper. "It's hard for kids to believe you have their best interest at heart if you can't respect what they care about."[13]

Above all, she cautions, don't attempt to incorporate the culture into youth organizing efforts if there is a limited understanding of it. "This is bound to fail. There are plenty of bad attempts at reaching youth on their own terms. Kids can smell a fake a mile away. Whatever you do, it's got to be real."

Youth culture is constantly changing. Unless one is totally immersed in it, it's hard to keep up. In each of the examples above, organizers address the culture question by allowing youth to develop their own materials and programs. That way, they are sure to be relevant and engaging to their peers.

Closing Thoughts

Developing good policy requires a careful examination of the larger context in which an issue "lives." Advocates must ask who profits from the problem and who pays. The answers to these questions provide clues to likely allies, opposition and targets. It's important to remember that no issue, no matter how critical or widespread, is without some entity that profits from it in some way.

Examining the context also means understanding relevant socio-demographic shifts. For example, what does it mean to try to enact school-based policies when, as in some inner-city school districts, more than half the students will be in a different school by the end of the school year? Too many initiatives are based on an inadequate understanding of the root causes of social problems. The result is misguided efforts that waste resources and solve nothing.

For example, state and federal organizations have invested funding in promotional campaigns to increase volunteerism. The premise of these campaigns is that people aren't volunteering because they aren't aware of volunteer opportunities. However, the fact is that the traditional volunteer base—mostly comprised of youth, stay-at-home mothers, and the elderly—is shrinking. More and more people in these demographic groups don't have as much time to volunteer because they are working to supplement their income. An initiative to increase volunteerism, given these realities, would look very different from a simple public awareness campaign. It must address the fundamental and structural barriers to participation.

Good policies address these structural or systemic barriers that affect a community's quality of life. It is not enough to address a community's poor health status, for example, by fighting for more money for educational programs or a school curriculum on nutrition and fitness.

Advocates must investigate where and how food is available. How safe is the community for walking and other forms of outdoor recreation? Will people who work all day be safe if they take a walk at night? A policy that ignores these barriers can do little to affect the problem.

The process of grassroots policy development is a careful balance of grassroots organizing for "outside" advocacy and mastering the "inside game" of the policy process. For policies seeking regulation in the public interest, community support must be visible and widespread in order to overcome established biases in policymaking toward business interests. The organizing activities take precedence over the policy work because the priority must be to build power among the groups' constituencies. The policy should support and amplify the organizing work, not the other way around.

Through research and careful "listening" to community needs, groups can develop policy initiatives that help shift the balance of power toward community interests. This shift, if effective, tends to upset established interests, making opposition likely. As advocates, we cannot shy away from opposition; instead, we must prepare for it by continually engaging supporters in our initiatives in the widest and deepest possible way. This way, we engage *both the process and the policy itself* in the service of community change, the long-term goal.

American culture is full of stories of small elites and triumphant individuals supposedly making every important social change in history. We tell the story of one courageous Rosa Parks—but not the tale of thousands of others who made up the Montgomery Bus Boycott. History books report much about Roosevelt's New Deal but very little about the unemployed councils that organized and fought for such legislation.

Perhaps it's true, as Margaret Mead has said, that a "small group of thoughtful, committed people can change the world." But they will only be successful with the help of many more supporters and "co-conspirators" willing to make some contribution to the cause. Community organizing is often tedious and time consuming, but it's the only way to build the democratic base of support necessary to make a real difference.

COMMON STAGES IN THE DEVELOPMENT OF A POLICY INITIATIVE

Most initiatives go through a development process characterized by seven stages. These stages are not sequential per se, but tend to over-lap—more like a gradual spectrum than a straight line. Once an initiative is under way, groups often work at more than one stage at a time. For example, groups will continually "test the waters" (stage one) through-out the life of an initiative and use that feedback to refine and improve their work.

Effective initiatives rarely miss any of these stages in development. Poor initiatives often do. I've often heard groups say that they went ahead without much preparation because of some unique opportunity that just wouldn't wait. While the right timing can provide important levers for an initiative's success, usually groups that plunge ahead wish they had wait-ed and been better prepared. There's nothing like good preparation and solid organizing to help a group take better advantage of the opportuni-ties that exist—as well as create new ones.

It's also important to recognize that developing policy is a process of negotiation and compromise. It's always helpful to know about similar policy initiatives that have been enacted without legal challenge or, at least, upheld in court. When working on a policy for which there is little precedence, remember that local governments are often afraid to be the first jurisdiction to adopt a new, untested ordinance. For that reason, first ordinances are usually more conservatively written and less comprehen-sive in scope than those that follow. Without some precedence, making a case for a new policy can be tough—but not impossible. In any case, it helps to decide early on what you can give up and what's non-nego-tiable. Remember, though you can go back and make changes later, it's a lot easier to get it "right" the first time.

STAGE 1: TESTING THE WATERS

At this stage, most groups are focused on the problem and are just beginning to develop ideas for solutions. It is when that first sense emerges that something concrete can be done about an issue but no one is sure exactly what. Often, a number of approaches are "tested" and screened for community support, legality and likelihood of success. For example, when a San Diego community group organized in the wake of the shooting death of a local youth, their first target was broad gun control. After conducting research on the legislative remedies available to them, however, they decided to focus on a ban of junk guns—and ways to regulate bullets locally. A key lesson: the coalition was flexible, researched their options, and made choices that were both informed and in line with member goals.

STAGE 2: DEFINING THE INITIATIVE

Once the primary issue is defined, it must be refined into a clear, practical policy initiative. An initiative is a planned set of activities, with clear goals and objectives, that a group will undertake to address some part of the issue. The best initiatives come out of residents articulating their "ideal" policy and then looking for the best mechanisms for bringing their vision into reality. The Coalition on Alcohol Outlet Issues wanted fewer liquor stores in Oakland and better regulation of those in operation. In their ideal policy, they wanted store owners, not public funds, to pay for enforcement. They took their idea to the city council, which then instructed staff to find a way. They did. The ordinance that resulted requires merchants to pay higher conditional-use permit fees to support an augmented regulatory structure.

STAGE 3: STRATEGY AND ANALYSIS

Once the initiative has been identified, groups conduct what is known as a "power analysis" to identify targets, allies, opponents and other factors that will be important in the campaign. Often, the initiative is refined further in light of this information. Living-wage coalitions, for example, decided to omit construction work from their initiatives in deference to their existing prevailing wage provisions as a strategic and political consideration (see page 62).

STAGE 4: DIRECT ISSUE ORGANIZING

Informed by the power analysis and strategic planning, the organizing begins. In city or countywide campaigns without a neighborhood focus, organizing is usually done through outreach to other organizations. For example, much of the organizing for living-wage campaigns focused on getting unions, advocacy organizations and affected (unorganized) employees to work on the issue. Neighborhood-oriented campaigns tend to conduct more canvassing operations. In Los Angeles, the Community Coalition for Substance Abuse Prevention and Treatment has organizers go door-to-door and hosts house parties as neighborhood meetings. They focus on neighborhoods with problem liquor stores in order to build a solid base of support among those most affected by the issue. It is during this stage that media work also begins in earnest.

STAGE 5: IN THE BELLY OF "THE BEAST"

At some point in every initiative, advocates must meet with policymakers and begin the long process of getting the policy enacted. This stage is characterized by intensive work with city or county staff, including nego- tiations and accountability sessions. It is important to stay focused on the group's initial goals during this phase, as it is easy to get caught up in the politics of the bureaucracy. Working with policymakers is an "inside" game, but it need not mean getting disconnected from grassroots sup- port. As veteran organizer Greg Akili says, "Don't start to talk like them or take on their ways. If you do you'll confuse the people you're working with and you become untrustworthy. Stay connected. Always go in groups and rotate the people who attend the meetings so that you build leadership and confidence."[5]

STAGE 6: VICTORY AND DEFENSE

If an initiative is enacted, celebration and evaluation are definitely in order. However, for most ordinances, soon after the partying is over, the litigation begins. Prepare for the possibility of litigation at the beginning of the initiative and be ready to play an active role in any legal action, even if the local government (and not your group) is the defendant. Some organizations, like the Los Angeles Community Coalition and the Coalition on Alcohol Outlet Issues, got intervenor status in legal action directed toward their city government. Baltimore's Citywide Liquor Coalition made sure their attorney worked closely with the city attorney throughout the process, carefully crafting public testimony with an eye toward building a strong public record in preparation for the inevitable litigation that would follow passage of the policy.

STAGE 7: ENFORCEMENT

After the policy is enacted and clear of court hurdles, the work begins to get the new law enforced. For initiatives with powerful opposition, nego- tiation continues around issues like the timeline for implementing the policy, interpretation of particular clauses, and fitting the new policy in with other staffing priorities. It is important to maintain grassroots involvement throughout this process.

ALL STAGES ARE IMPORTANT

One common mistake is to launch policy initiatives without any prepara- tion or prior analysis, as outlined above in the first three stages of devel- opment, before direct advocacy begins. On the other hand, numerous policy initiatives skip stage four and therefore suffer from inadequate grassroots support because not enough attention was paid to community organizing. Advocates in this case often go directly to stage five, working with policymakers, without grassroots support or even public awareness of their efforts, in hopes that policymakers will be swayed by the "sensibility" of their initiative. However, policy is not about sensibility as much as it is about interests. Advocates must never assume support based on the logic of their argument or the strength of a personal relationship. They must marshal the voices of the most interested parties behind them.

One coalition in a small town in the Midwest took their initiative directly to a local policymaker without building support, identifying allies or even working through the details of their initiative. Their idea seemed straightforward and simple: to have their local hospital keep track of alcohol-related gun trauma. They were completely caught by surprise when the hospital administrator did not agree to simply enact the policy at their request. It was an honest mistake. The group had a warm relationship with the administrator but had not thought through the implications of such a policy on staff resources. By doing the necessary preparation, groups can effectively manage these issues and plan accordingly.

5

TALKING POLICY:

Media and the Message

Whoever controls the flow of information dictates our perceptions and perspectives; whoever controls the news shapes our destiny.

—GEORGE CLINTON, MUSICIAN AND FUNK PHILOSOPHER [1]

If public policy is the official social contract, news is the "official story." News confers legitimacy upon an issue, sets the public agenda and drives public discourse. What the story is and how that story is covered will largely determine public sentiment—especially among public officials. One poignant example of this influence was the difference between media coverage of the Ruby Ridge incident in 1992 (a stand-off and shoot-out between militia members and the Bureau of Alcohol, Tobacco and Firearms, or ATF, at Ruby Ridge in Idaho) and the rash of church burnings in mostly southern black communities that received media coverage in 1996.

The national media thoroughly covered Ruby Ridge and related incidents, developing more than 500 individual stories on the stand-off, subsequent shooting and its aftermath. The church burnings, though they took place over a longer period of time (recent burnings have taken place at least from 1990 to the present), received much less attention—fewer than 100 individual stories. Ruby Ridge coverage focused on wrongdoing by ATF and on human-interest stories about the non-ATF participants. Coverage of the church burnings, with few exceptions, focused on whether the arsons were racially motivated, youthful pranks, or were the work of church members burning their own churches down. Coverage in both cases spurred congressional hearings.

The 1995 hearings for Ruby Ridge took many days; agents, government officials and victims were all called in. The half-day hearing held on the church burnings called few victims and questioned no FBI officials charged with investigating the arsons, in spite of local accusations that law enforcement personnel were harassing residents instead of properly investigating the crimes. The congressional committee tacitly refused to look into these accusations and focused instead on the only question raised by the media: Were the arsons racially motivated? The committee left the few hours of testimony on the church burnings satisfied that this was not the case.

The New Media Existentialism

The revolution will not be televised. It will be live.

—GIL SCOTT HERRON, SINGER AND POET[2]

How do you know you are really in a "movement"? Is it because one thousand people showed up at a rally? Or because your work was on the evening news? For more and more activists, the answer is the latter. Media names and legitimizes movements, making it easier for groups to recruit, fundraise and institutionalize after receiving coverage. This is a relatively new but important phenomenon that has its roots in the rise of television news in the 1960s. Media's extensive coverage of certain political movements during that period, such as the Vietnam War resistance and the Civil Rights Movement, helped to establish public awareness and support for these efforts. Today, advocates continue to depend on the media for a great deal of their public awareness efforts. Unfortunately, however, due to a variety of factors, the media are not as cooperative or as interested as they once were.

Advocacy events—even large ones—no longer attract much news coverage. One reason is that there are many more events with larger and larger numbers of participants. This makes one rally hard to distinguish from another and frame as newsworthy. Given this reality, it may make sense to think of rallies and other large-scale events more as a method for organizing people and building enthusiasm than for attracting news media. Building support is still a very important outcome—cameras rolling or not.

TOUGH COMPETITION

During the 1960s, the media portrayed public-interest advocacy efforts quite positively and their opposition as wrong headed. Prior to 1975, in many cases the opposition was less visible, and what opposition did step forward was much less media savvy. Politically conservative groups or business interests had not yet learned to engage in advocacy tactics. It seems these groups were caught completely off guard by the grassroots activism so prevalent at the time.

Today, however, competition for the airwaves and the streets is much tougher. Well-funded and media-savvy conservatives use slick public relations firms to develop both media and organizing campaigns to promote their issues. Now the public-interest advocacy community is the one caught off guard and not well organized enough to mount a compelling opposition.

And third, the media, too, are different. There were many more independent media outlets in 1968 than there are today. Independent media, especially "alternative" newspapers, were then in a period of great expansion.[3] Even the ownership of corporate media was less centralized. Today, fewer than two dozen companies own virtually all of the mainstream media outlets in the United States.[4]

Today, news media are dedicating more of their time to promoting the business interests of their owners. The industry term for this practice is *synergy*. The American Broadcasting Company, now owned by Disney, offers a sad case in point. Since Disney purchased the television network, ABC's morning news program, "Good Morning America," has dedicated several segments to Disney products and programs—a practice not seen prior to the sale.

The combination of a shrinking number of increasingly interconnected media outlets and louder, better organized opposition has left advocates with fewer places to tell their stories—and fewer sympathetic sources to tell them to. Despite the right wing's reflexive labeling of media professionals as part of the "liberal elite," recent polls of reporters' attitudes reflect an increasing political conservatism which, coupled with the media's greater emphasis on supporting business interests, greatly narrows the air time for progressive political debate.[5]

THE SHRINKING INSTITUTIONAL VOICE

In addition to allotting less *time* for political discussion, the news is also offering a narrower *range* of ideas. By choosing the voices and faces that represent the various sides of an issue, the news media determine the poles of debate. The narrower the distance between the two sides represented in a story, the more marginalized opinions outside of those poles become. A case in point: A large California daily newspaper ran a story in 1996 comparing "environmentally safe" cleaning fluids with standard cleaning fluids. The story quoted two sources: the Clorox

Corporation and a research organization that receives Clorox funding (a fact omitted from the story). Given the narrow range of opinion, the story's conclusion was as could be expected, if illogical: lemon juice and chlorine bleach pose about the same risk to the environment, but bleach cleans better. An activist's follow-up call to the reporter revealed that she did not quote an environmental group in the story because she did not think an environmental group could be objective on the issue. She also didn't think the research group's funding was germane to the story because, she noted, they had done "solid research on a wide range of issues." She did not consider the fact that on this issue they may be heavily biased by their funding source. Further, the reporter did not even apply common sense, as a simple taste test would have revealed the difference in toxicity between lemons and chlorine.

Despite the fact that there are plenty of good reporters, this reporter, unfortunately, is not atypical. It is increasingly difficult for advocates to be included in the very stories that cover the issues on which they are working. Instead of being perceived as experts, they are ruled out as subjective and biased.

This bias against organizational sources is transforming public affairs coverage in several ways. First, there is the rise of "pulse" stories. Formerly reserved for background and "sidebars," stories that feature only uninvolved, "regular people" for comment are gaining popularity as the main feature article or news segment on a particular issue. Experts are replaced with the "person in the street," whose opinion is thought to be of more interest to the consumers of news.

Another effect is the exclusion of advocates from opinion-based public affairs programming. While there is a preponderance of business and government officials as guests on these programs, in more and more programs there are no guests at all. Increasingly, public affairs programs, such as the Sunday morning talk shows, feature only the opinions of other reporters.[6]

The result of these practices is that the poles of debate are narrowed until various pro-business interests, usually from academia, corporations or the public policy arena, are talking to each other. Every other view is marginalized and made invisible. As a study of ABC's program "Nightline" has found:

> "Nightline" helps to set limits on public discourse. The range of guests helps to define the limits of legitimate debate and stakes out the limits of dissenting opinion. Most important, the process of exclusion plays a role in delegitimizing positions:

voices that are regularly and systematically excluded from "Nightline" seem to have no role in legitimate public discussion.[7]

As a consequence of this narrowed coverage, public awareness and understanding of public affairs has decreased, as Robert McChesney points out in *Corporate Media and the Threat to Democracy*: "Indeed, in what stands as perhaps the most damning statement one could make about the news media, some studies have suggested that the more a person consumes commercial news, the less capable that person is of understanding politics or public affairs."[8]

Yet, it is with this compromised understanding that many public policy decisions are made. Recently, the dismantling of affirmative action and welfare programs, the direction of drug policy and the needs of public schools are but a few of the important policy issues whose debates have received narrow, superficial coverage in mainstream media. Advocates working on these issues have to combat misinformation *before* they can even begin to advance their message (if they get the opportunity). Such double duty in the face of the ever-shrinking news hole is daunting indeed.

As troubling as these trends are, there is still hope. Strategies that address both how media operate and how advocates work with media can help public-interest advocates effectively address these challenges. The stakes are high. Without serious media planning and cultivation, we may find ourselves locked out of our own debate.

The Art of Media Advocacy

More and more, policy decisions are determined by public perceptions of an issue, and those perceptions are the product of news media. Therefore, media coverage is a key factor in building support for advocacy initiatives—and advocates must learn to use it effectively. Effective media advocacy is simply using the news to influence public opinion and affect the terms of debate. It's hard to think about being proactive in the newsmaking process but, with the proper preparation and planning, any savvy group can participate in shaping the news.

How does the right story "happen"? That has a lot to do with what kind of information advocates are prepared to provide the public. And that, in turn, has to do with the ways that organizations are prepared to interact with the media. It's more than just being ready for an interview. It is a basic issue of having the infrastructure (e.g., fact sheets, mailing lists, materials, staffing, etc.) to effectively support media-related work.

The first step in developing an organizational infrastructure for media advocacy is learning the media terrain. Framing an issue without first monitoring media coverage of it is like driving cross country and having no idea what direction to go, what month it is, or what the weather will be. Good media advocacy requires some surveying of the media landscape and a system for tracking coverage and media outlets.

Start with the many published media lists available through bookstores or nonprofit associations. For example, *Editor and Publisher* puts out an annual yearbook of media outlets. Those media outlets that are important to a group's efforts should be called to get the names of key contacts. Who is the main reporter on health issues or environmental issues? Who should be contacted with a public service announcement? Routine calls should be made to update lists, as personnel move frequently.

Try to track coverage of your issue and related topics at least monthly. Clipping services (both electronic and paper) are useful for tracking newspaper coverage. Some electronic services will also track broadcast transcripts uploaded on databases or on the World Wide Web. Many local papers, especially ethnic and other community presses, are not a part of these services. It makes sense to regularly monitor (i.e., read, watch, subscribe to) key outlets in your area.

Pay special attention to your issue's placement in papers or on broadcast news (is it the lead story? the last?); who's quoted, how they are quoted and how much; whether the reporter had a grasp of the issue's complexity/importance; and the overall angle or frame of the story. If there are no stories on the issue, look for coverage on related issues. For example, if there are no recent stories on teen suicide, what kind of coverage are teens getting in general?

Too many groups attempt to reach the media without properly defining an issue. An issue is the overarching concern that drives your initiative (see Chapter 4), whether it's a problem or vision statement. Issues should reflect the mission, core values and concerns of the organization or coalition—and should incorporate an institutional angle. That is, the description of an issue should identify ways that institutional actors (government, corporations, etc.) have an affect on the issue, and should develop strategies to make institutional change for the better. This is important, as a key tenet of media advocacy is *advocacy for change at the institutional level*—not marketing changes in individual behavior. Here are some examples of issue statements:

Not-So-Good Issue Statement: Teen violence is a problem; we have to get teens to leave guns alone. No institutional angle here; no opportunities to advocate for institutional change. In this construction of the issue, there's only room for education programs that seek to market new behaviors to youth. Of course, education programs are important, but they are not advocacy.

Good Issue Statement from a **Problem** *Perspective: Teen violence is a problem; we have to address where young people get their weapons.*

Good Issue Statement from a **Vision** *Perspective:* We can have a safe and healthy community for our young people if we expand opportunities for healthy, alternative activities.

Once an issue is defined, the group is ready to identify an action or initiative to address the issue. This is the most important step in preparing for media advocacy because it will define what you communicate about and to whom. Identifying an initiative requires an honest assessment of the group's strengths and weaknesses, the political climate, and thorough research of the available options (see Chapter 4).

Know who you are talking to. Most media advocacy is focused on getting the message to the initiative's target because that is who has the power to enact the desired change. In some cases, groups use media advocacy to mobilize supporters as a preliminary step to targeting policymakers. Although media can support organizing goals, it can never be a substitute for organizing. That's why most groups shape their media strategy to target policymakers.

Once the target is chosen, research how they get their information. Most elected officials and other gatekeepers read the editorial pages of local newspapers to gauge community concerns. Television news also helps set the public agenda and affects the "public conversation" on a particular issue.

Know what you're saying. Now you are ready to take the final step in preparation: developing a message. A message is not a sound bite or a slogan (although it can help shape them). It is the overarching theme that neatly frames your initiative for your target audience. Messages should be relatively short, easy-to-understand, emotive and visual. The message should reflect the hard work and research that went into developing the initiative and should be supportive of the overall strategy.

The California Wellness Foundation's Violence Prevention Initiative (VPI) invested significant resources in developing messages on youth violence. They invested in public opinion research (including polling and focus groups) that uncovered critical information that would guide their media effort. First, they found that most people did not know that handguns were the number-one killer of kids in California. Their research indicated that once people knew, they were much more likely to support gun control. The polling and focus groups also helped them to figure out which segments of the population tended to agree with them the most. This allowed them to prioritize and focus their resources.

Gun control is no easy issue. Armed with the data and a strong media plan, the foundation believed that if they could shift the discourse on guns from a "rights" issue to a public health issue, they would have a better chance of winning against some awesome opponents: the gun lobby.

Their message was the straightforward, simple message that worked so well in focus groups: "Handguns are the number-one killer of kids in California." With this message, they supported a statewide campaign to limit guns and increase gun safety through the enactment of dozens of state and local policies. They won legislation mandating trigger locks for guns, banning junk guns, and restricting the number and concentration of gun outlets.[9]

It's best to test messages on friends and co-workers—especially those who are not familiar with your issue. Colleagues working on similar issues are another good resource. Listen carefully to feedback: Did the message convey the importance of your issue? Did the listener understand what you are advocating and why? Keeping your target in mind, use the input to help shape and refine your message.

FRAMING THE MESSAGE

Every frame defines the issue, explains who is responsible, and suggests potential solutions.

—CHARLOTTE RYAN, MEDIA SCHOLAR AND ACTIVIST[10]

Good messages are affective and strike the receiver as making good sense. In the case of advocacy campaigns, they also must give people a sense that something can and will be done about the issue at hand. Framing is the art and handiwork of ensuring that the message works as intended.

In the seminal book, *Is Anyone Responsible? How Television Frames Political Issues*, Shanto Iyengaar examined how television news framed important issues like crime and poverty and its effects on viewer perception of those issues. He divided stories into roughly two categories: *episodic* and *thematic,* with most news stories having more of one characteristic than the other.[11]

Episodic stories are the most common news stories. They focus on individuals who illustrate or individualize a particular issue. For example, an episodic news story on unemployment will feature interviews with unemployed people, pictures of people standing in line and perhaps an interview with someone who recently found a job. It's called episodic because it explores a single episode in the life of the story. None (or very little) of the history or context that shapes the issue is included.

According to Iyengaar, when people watch episodic news stories they focus on the individuals and forget about the context. They are disconnected from any sense that there may be a solution to the problem and that institutions have some responsibility for addressing the problem. Further, viewers have a tendency to *blame the people portrayed* in the story for the problem without any other information to go on.[12]

During the coverage of welfare repeal in 1995 there were numerous stories featuring women telling compelling personal stories about what the policy changes would do to their lives. It made riveting journalism but bad framing for policy. Too often, the news story is all the information many viewers have on a given issue. Without a sense of the forces that brought these women to this point, viewers were left with only two choices for action: make donations to the women portrayed, or blame their lack of achievement on bad luck or lack of initiative.

Another common pitfall for activists is to pitch episodic stories featuring exceptional people who have triumphed over great odds. The idea is to put a nice "face" on a problem to demonstrate the possibility of rehabilitation and change. New York metropolitan media featured a news story in 1997 on a high school valedictorian who was homeless. The stories marveled at how the youngster lived on city buses and on the streets but still managed to keep his grades high. Instead of investigating why the young man was homeless, looking into the lives of other homeless children, and discussing what could be done, the stories praised the young man's tenacity and effectively implied, "Why can't all kids be valedictorians if this kid is?"

The story probably didn't move many people to care about the plight of homeless children in New York. It did move people to care about the young man in the story. The focus on individuals, as discussed in Chapter 1, is an important core value in this country, but advocates must overcome this bias and frame stories from a "thematic" perspective.

Thematic stories deal with the systemic and institutional issues that form the context of a story. A thematic story on welfare repeal would talk about the availability of jobs, child care, and public transportation to job sites for former recipients. In this kind of story, a woman might recount her four-hour bus ride to work or lament the fact that she only sees her child while he's sleeping. It may mean gathering data on whether there are enough jobs for everyone. Such a story might even question why child rearing is not considered work and explore the history of the issue.

Thematic stories engage viewers while giving them a sense of the history and context of a story. They hold institutions and policies responsible for the current state of affairs and offer a sense of the alternatives. At bottom, good thematic framing is about how the stories themselves are constructed. That construction is the heart of framing.

Framing is the process by which facts, opinions and images are packaged together to become a news story. There are many ways to frame a story. Media scholar Dr. Lori Dorfman often likens framing to the view from a speeding train while one looks out of the window. As the train speeds by, the window frames the landscape—that is, it arranges the images so that some are more prominent than others. The moving train imagery is an apt description of how news media move through issues. There often isn't time for detail and long-term study, but with purposeful planning and good information management, advocates can greatly influence this process.[13]

Framing for Access

Getting media attention means getting that moving train to stop and pay attention to our issue. This is called *framing for access*. There are many techniques for framing a story to make it accessible to media.

Controversy, conflict, injustice. The news media are in the storytelling business. Highlighting these aspects makes stories interesting. While you might frame the story with a personal angle showing the effect of controversy, conflict or injustice on individuals, be sure to bring the story back to the institutional reasons that people are caught in the situation.

Irony or uniqueness. What's different about this story? What will make viewers sit up and pay attention? What is new in this news?

Population of interest. Media outlets are businesses that must reach consumers in order to stay profitable. Oftentimes, some demographic groups (and therefore, stories that potentially appeal to them) are of greater interest than others. Call the advertising departments of your local media outlets for their package to prospective advertisers. These materials are free and often specify an outlet's target markets. See if you have a match between your issue and their consumers.

Significant, serious. Although this is often subjective, any story affecting large numbers of people meets this criterion. For example, a story broadcasting the outbreak of lethal food poisoning or a widespread banking crisis would be serious enough to warrant media attention.

Breakthrough, anniversary, milestone. Something new and amazing—like a discovery or new drug, or the commemoration of an important event. Tobacco control activists, for example, pegged a 1994 study on youth and tobacco to the 30th anniversary of the first Surgeon General's report on smoking with good results.

Local peg, breaking news. Piggybacking on a news story that is already getting media attention can be an effective strategy. For example, advocates artfully used the O.J. Simpson case to raise public awareness of the tragedy of domestic violence.

Good pictures. If a picture is worth a thousand words and the average media bite is seven seconds, developing compelling visuals that illustrate your perspective is critical. Moreover, visuals operate at the level of emotion and are accessible across different languages and literacy levels. Give serious thought to the colors, symbols and backdrop of any visuals you present. All media, including print media, need good visuals for their stories. Some groups provide balloons to demonstrators or meet in front of dramatic backdrops. Others opt for more emotional visuals like candlelight vigils or deteriorating neighborhoods in order to provide news media with some direct experience of the issues advocates seek to address. Choose the pictures that best illustrate your message.

Framing for Content

Once you have the media's attention, actively shape the story by providing information, interviews, sources and visuals that will effectively frame the story accurately and from a public health or social justice perspective. This element of framing is known as *framing for content.* Framing for content increases the odds that the story is told in a way that reflects the public interest perspective of the issue.

One way to think of framing for content is to imagine each story as a blank comic strip. The reporter or producer must tell a story with a few words illustrated by a picture. Stories have more than one side, so advocates must anticipate and even suggest "characters" for the entire "strip." There will likely be members of the opposition, authentic voices or people who are personally affected by the issue, and experts with important information to provide. Pitching a good story requires paying attention to the whole picture and not just your angle. It also means remembering that the goal is getting a good story, not being quoted. A quote is the most superficial level of impact an advocate can have on a story. It is far more important to influence the story with good, accurate and accessible background information and to refer to other good sources (including your opposition). Providing both sides of the story will increase your credibility with the media.

Translate individual problem to social issue. The first step in framing is to make sure that what you say is consistent with your approach. It's hard to justify an environmental approach to an issue if all the media interviews frame it from an individual perspective. Further, a social issue affecting large numbers of people is news, one individual problem is not. Placing an issue in its social context helps others to see why it is important and newsworthy.

Assign primary responsibility. Again consistency is key. If the issue is tobacco sales to kids, it's hard to justify a new ordinance if spokespeople assign primary responsibility for the problem to parents. Framing for content means framing your message in ways that support your initiative goal and explain to others why the target you chose is the right entity to address the issue.

Present solution. The message should clearly articulate what the initiative can address. For example, the solution offered for youth access to tobacco is to make it harder for merchants to profit from youth smoking.

Make practical/policy appeal. This is where the initiative comes in. It should be communicated as practical, fair, legal, affordable and the right thing to do. It should also preempt the opposition by addressing their likely criticism—including economic arguments.

Tailor to the audience. Remember who you are trying to reach in each case. Communities are fragmented with lots of different interests and concerns. Tailor your message to your audience, which is first and foremost usually your target.

FACING THE BARRIERS

Media advocacy, when conventionally done, requires a tremendous amount of time to cultivate reporters' interests. These relationships are often built through personal contact with reporters in common social settings, through work relationships or by becoming a regular source for stories or background. In many communities, meeting reporters under any of these conditions can be difficult. Some media outlets don't regularly cover certain communities (especially communities of color) or only cover them in very narrow ways (i.e., crime stories). Studies such as the groundbreaking work, *What Color Is the News?* by Erna Smith show that numerous factors, including lack of staff diversity in media outlets and deeply ingrained patterns of segregation in living and work patterns overall, are barriers to coverage.[14]

Communities also struggle with what happens when they are covered. Sometimes news stories are so negative and defamatory that groups would rather just leave media alone. In any case, it is a wise group that weighs their media outreach carefully against any possible damage attention from the media could inflict.

However, these difficult conditions provide fertile soil for creative media advocacy. Careful, adept use of sound bites, work to engage the full spectrum of media (including religious and ethnic media), and the employment of attention-getting press events have helped groups overcome these barriers with aplomb. For example, during the Campaign for Justice for Aaron Williams discussed in Chapter 4, activists held colorful events with music and poetry to attract the media. They also wrote pieces for publication in community newspapers and appeared on local radio programming, including one popular Sunday morning show with a youthful, hip hop format.

Having a clear sense of your audience and their stake in the issue is critical to media advocacy success. In media advocacy, there are generally two kinds of audiences: the primary audience—or target—which is the decisionmaker or decisionmaking body (public or private) to be influenced or pressured to change, and the secondary audience—potential allies to be mobilized to help pressure the target. Effective coalitions chart each potential ally's and target's self-interest, depth of concern and risk in supporting the initiative in order to shape an effective message to draw them in—or neutralize them. Of course, media advocacy is not the same as organizing a power base, but it can really help when integrated into an overall organizing strategy.

CHOOSING THE RIGHT TARGET

Effective advocates often employ a two-pronged strategy that simultaneously shames targets and catalyzes action at the community level. Successful groups take great care to choose targets they have some degree of power over, and to exploit targets' vulnerabilities in the media. In a campaign against X brand cigarettes, for example, activists chose to target the small company that manufactured the cigarettes.

As described in Chapter 4, X was a cigarette brand that many activists believed appropriated the strong, positive sentiment that young African Americans have for Malcolm X in order to sell cigarettes. Based in Massachusetts, the brand was manufactured by a small company, Star Tobacco Corporation, and marketed and distributed by another small enterprise, Duffy Distributors. The packaging, marketing and low price seemed a lethal weapon in the tobacco industry's efforts to hook more young African Americans.

Mobilization for the X campaign began when Brenda Bell-Caffee, director of the California African American Tobacco Education Network (AATEN), saw a message posted on the SCARCNet website. She immediately alerted the National Association of African Americans for Positive Imagery (NAAAPI), which developed a strategy for tackling the issue. After some research, the group found that the two small companies involved were more vulnerable targets than any relevant public agencies. The message was, therefore, crafted to mobilize pressure and publicly shame these companies. As part of the campaign, the group issued the companies a 10-day deadline to withdraw the brand or face widespread negative publicity.

Media played a critical role in getting the word out. Articles on X brand appeared in more than 100 newspapers nationwide during the two-week campaign. The group worked both African-American and corporate-owned media outlets and, despite pressure to do otherwise, kept the focus on the company—not on the stereotypical story of pathology and failing among African-American youth. Bell-Caffee had strong relationships with publications owned by African Americans through her years as a reporter for the *Sacramento Observer* and found the *Observer* and other newspapers in the West Coast Publishers'

Association (a regional association of African American-owned newspapers) particularly receptive.

One day after the deadline, Duffy Distributors issued a statement that—without any admission of wrongdoing—detailed their commitment to withdraw the brand. The group's focused media efforts, and the fact that their targets were such small companies ill prepared for such pressure, contributed to X's quick demise.

GAINING ACCESS

Bringing attention to communities that don't fit the media's primary market demographic is a special challenge. Routine media advocacy approaches (i.e., cultivating and leveraging press relationships) simply aren't as effective when you are not the audience this outlet is trying to reach. Some of the many reasons are mentioned above, including the lack of race and class diversity in most newsrooms, and the fact that, for low-income communities in particular, there are real barriers to developing relationships with journalists.

Another increasingly important factor is the rise of market-oriented (or sales-driven) reporting. That is, reporting specifically geared to engage a market or demographic segment (such as housewives, parents over 40, etc.). The result: more focus on affluent suburbs and less on communities with less buying power. For communities of color (and communities with significant numbers of poor people) this means even less of an opportunity to tell stories that affect their communities.

Given this sparse attention, advocates have to develop creative access strategies. Press events that mobilize community support and draw out an issue's more controversial elements are a cornerstone in attracting media. One early strategy in the effort to regulate alcohol and tobacco billboards in Chicago and New York involved painting them over (or whitewashing) at highly publicized gatherings. Reporters came out to cover these colorful acts of civil disobedience—especially if they thought they could catch an arrest on film.

Other coalitions organized large-scale marches and demonstrations. In Detroit, councilwoman Alberta Tinsley Williams' Coalition Against Billboard Advertising of Alcohol and Tobacco (CABAAT) mounted highly theatrical community marches and rallies. More recently, in efforts to oppose Camel Menthol cigarettes, CABAAT staged sit-ins in retail establishments to draw coverage and further politicize the issue.

Milwaukee Makes Press a Picnic

When the Milwaukee Coalition Against Alcohol and Drug Abuse (MCAADA) decided to take on the overconcentration of billboards in its predominantly African-American and Latino Center City, they knew they needed media attention if their initiative was to succeed. After all, much of Milwaukee ignored the problems of this area. It was almost as if their neighborhoods were invisible to the press and policymakers.

The group wanted to do a community-wide billboard count, an activity that would encourage family participation and build awareness of the problem, while giving the coalition hard data on the issue. While a count could engage hundreds of volunteers, how could it capture the attention of the media? MCAADA found the answer by executing the count as a one-day event.

Recruiting large numbers of volunteers to form carpool teams, the coalition divided the area into smaller regions for easy counting. The event started with a rousing rally at a neighborhood park with local "celebrities." Reporters were provided a guided bus tour of the area to observe the activities—and the issue—close up. Results gathered by teams were posted on the park's scoreboard. These results not only tallied findings, they also contrasted billboard placement in Center City neighborhoods with the total number of billboards throughout the city. At the end of the day, final results were announced and MCAADA showed participants and the press alike their appreciation with a picnic spread and music.

Their strategy was hugely successful, garnering coverage on virtually every media outlet in the area. Thanks to MCAADA's creativity and organizing efforts, billboard regulation was on the news and on the public policy agenda.

USING MEDIA IN MANY FORMS

In addition to creative events, advocates get the word out by working with a wide range of media—much of it outside of mainstream press. They work with institutional publications (i.e., newsletters and bulletins) to garner hard news coverage—a real departure from these organs' traditional role mainly as venues for promoting events to members. To facilitate placement, advocates often write and package camera-ready news stories for easy insertion into a publication. Faith publications are an important resource in this regard.

Another important source for coverage has been "alternative" media—weekly local newspapers, radio and cable programming that are committed to covering social issues. As advocates usually frame their issues within larger social contexts, they are well prepared to work effectively with these outlets to develop more in-depth coverage.

INTEGRATING MEDIA INTO THE ORGANIZING CONTEXT

Media advocacy is one tool to support social change. It cannot make change in and of itself. Effective use of media advocacy requires that advocates have a clear organizing strategy, of which outreach to media is only a part. Think of media advocacy as a microphone. It amplifies your message and gets you heard. It can even capture your message and help make it a matter of record, but your message must support your goals and objectives. If it doesn't, it's worthless.

KNOWING WHEN TO WALK AWAY

There are also occasions when it's better to leave the media alone.

The Coalition Against Uptown Cigarettes quickly formed after news spread of RJ Reynolds' plan to test-market Uptown cigarettes—a brand targeting African Americans—in Philadelphia. The Coalition was an extremely diverse gathering of health, religious and community organizations led by African Americans working in the Philadelphia community. They held their coalition together by agreeing on a number of basic principles, which included organizing broadly in the African-American community, placing the focus on RJR and not on other African Americans or African-American organizations that might be on the "wrong side" of the issue, and making their effort a *local* one to stop RJR from test-marketing the product in Philadelphia. Their primary goal was to mobilize the African-American community around this issue.

With these principles understood, the Coalition appeared to use the media primarily as a tool to mobilize their community. Local media were deemed more important than national media, and local media outlets that "spoke to" African Americans were more important still. Even though this second set of principles was clear, it still was not easy to abide by it.

Immediately after the first Coalition meeting, the American Cancer Society (an Uptown Coalition member) received a call from the *New York Times* requesting a list of the organizations that had joined the Coalition. For some, this seemed an important opportunity for publicity. After all, this was the *New York Times,* the newspaper of record for this country. For others, it seemed too soon to publish the list.

The Coalition, at that time, consisted primarily of groups in the classic tobacco control movement (i.e., American Cancer Society and the American Lung Association) and was not yet representative of the broader African-American community. Most African-American organizations needed time to go through their organization's endorsement process to be able to lend their formal support to the effort. There was concern that the resulting story would be that this coalition was made up of "the same old players" and that the issue had gained little attention among broader segments of the African-American community.

The group decided to take their chances on waiting to release the list at an upcoming press conference when more member organizations could be announced. "And sure enough," says Coalition leader Charyn Sutton, "we got other African-American organizations and the *Times* didn't go away. They understood."

The group faced a similar decision when ABC's "Good Morning America" called requesting that a representative come on the show to debate a marketing expert on the Uptown issue. The marketing expert was African American. It was strictly against the Coalition's principles to engage in any activity that would pit them against other African Americans or African-American institutions in public. It was a clear call for the Coalition, but less so for other tobacco-control activists nationwide, who saw the appearance as a good opportunity to promote the Uptown issue to a wider audience. The Coalition was firm and the answer was no.

In addition to turning down "Good Morning America," the Coalition also turned down other national news programs, including "The McNeil-Lehrer News Hour," because the Coalition's focus was on the local community. "We would go to a local newspaper before we would go national," said Sutton. "Even though there was more glamour in the national media, it was a diversion. Our task was the local piece. Our audience was in Philadelphia. The test market was in Philadelphia and if we could win it, we would win it in Philadelphia."[15]

The Uptown media effort was part of an overall plan to mobilize a community. The media strategy was driven by campaign goals, not the other way around. Campaign goals informed the Coalition's choice of audience, media outlets, and even the composition of the Coalition and its leadership—and it did not veer from those choices. This kind of clarity in goal-setting and refusal to dilute its vision was key to the Coalition's success in keeping Uptown cigarettes from ever seeing the light of day.

THE IMPORTANCE AND THE DILEMMA
OF THE AUTHENTIC VOICE

The media are often interested in putting an "authentic voice" or face on a story to give it human interest. From an organizing perspective, part of a new, flexible definition of expertise requires a thorough examination of who portrays that voice. On a basic level, this is an issue of leadership development, mentoring, and support of spokespeople who have not traditionally played that role. It is important to provide opportunities for those who are most affected by a policy or problem to speak out on their own behalf. In fact, the act of speaking out on one's own issue (which is the highest goal of using an authentic voice) is an act of claiming power in itself.

Mothers Against Drunk Driving is a good example of how individuals can organize and use their position as authentic voices to make themselves heard on policy issues and gather personal strength in the face of tragedy. These women and men, as people with a direct stake in the outcome, advocate for alcohol policy to reduce drinking and driving. In this way, they use their experience to help others.

Of course, advocates must exercise caution in how they employ "victims" in their coalition building. Problems can arise when "authentic voices" are simply used for photo opportunities without any effort to integrate them into coalition efforts. Again, advocates must be vigilant in their endeavor to forge a broad, inclusive definition of expertise that allows for the greatest range of human expression and creativity.

DEFENSIVE FRAMING

Sometimes it is hard to draw media attention in spite of the best efforts. When this happens, it may be time for *defensive framing*. Defensive framing is a set of tactics designed to reverse consistently negative media portrayals. It is a strategy for dealing with difficult media and should only be employed in those cases. Occasional misquotes or quotes taken out of context, although troublesome, are not enough to justify a defensive framing strategy. That's why defensive planning should always start with an accurate and honest assessment of the group or issue's coverage. Don't forget to look critically at your organization's or coalition's role. Some key questions include:

- Did we adequately prepare for interviews?
- Did we contact authors, reporters and/or editorial boards when

negative stories or editorials were published or broadcast? Did we provide solid, credible information to counter these pieces?

- How strong is our opposition? What role do they play in coverage?
- Is coverage balanced and fair (even if we don't like it)?
- Are there certain outlets that are more *consistently* negative than others? Are there negative experiences with specific reporters?

Identify patterns of coverage. Spend some time monitoring recent media coverage to identify the extent and source of the damage. By reviewing a sample period, you can determine if there is a pattern of negative portrayals of the issue, a particular community, or your organization. Start with the last six months if there has been a lot of coverage. Review a longer period if there's been less. If coverage has taken a recent turn for the worse, review at least three months before and after the shift.

Once you've determined the extent and source of the damage, you are ready to develop a defensive framing plan. The following are some common challenges and effective counter-strategies. Remember, good strategies are formed by accurate assessments. Make sure you've done your homework. Your organization's particular problem may be one, none, or a combination of any of the following scenarios.

Stereotyping

The problem: Researchers have well documented that the news industry is as likely to fall prey to negative stereotypes of race, gender or cultural groups as any other segment in society. Unfortunately, such a slant can lead to scapegoating certain individuals or groups and using dehumanizing images that make framing stories from a broader public interest perspective difficult.[16]

In fact, racist stereotypes have so penetrated the national psyche that, as studies by Iyengaar show, the race of people portrayed in a news story is the single most important factor in predicting how viewers will react to that story. When the people portrayed are of color, viewers tend to blame the person in the story for the problem at the story's focus—despite story content indicating the contrary. For example, if the news story portrays a black woman being mistreated by a public agency, viewers will tend to blame the woman, not the agency. This tendency toward blame is even more pronounced when the person(s) in the story are African American. It's depressing news to be sure and recent studies by Dr. Frank Gilliam of UCLA only confirm that things have not changed. It will take serious work to turn them around.[17]

Counter-strategies: Start by documenting bias in your media outlets. This is a great project for community members—especially youth. The group, We Interrupt This Message, (see Appendix) can provide tracking forms and other tools. Once you have identified the bias, write letters of concern to the outlet and meet with key leadership in the targeted media to advocate for concrete steps for change (such as changes in hiring and editorial practices, attention to a broader range of stories, etc.). Follow up any meetings with continued letter-writing campaigns and press advisories to keep the issue on the front burner. Some groups release their findings directly to the media and then meet with outlets. How your organization proceeds will depend on your assessment of the political terrain. Remember, shaming outlets is only a means to the real end: changing the situation for the better.

They Just Don't Get It

The problem: They keep calling you anti-jobs, anti-alcohol—anti-anything but the pro-public interest group you are. Each time you spin your frame on policy and environmental causes, they ask more questions about families and individual responsibility.

Counter-strategies: This is an education campaign pure and simple. Start by practicing ways to clearly capture your perspective in neat, visual sound bites. Try messages out on people who are unfamiliar with your issue. You can peruse news stories to see how similar groups have framed these issues and borrow their techniques liberally. Once you've identified an effective message, put together a press packet with relevant data and other supporting information, along with the bios and contact information for people with diverse but supportive perspectives.

Some basic steps in repairing the damage:

1. Meet with key reporters and producers individually (when possible) to discuss your perspective away from the pressure of deadlines
2. Immediately call to provide feedback and give more information on both "good" and "bad" stories and mail the press packet described above as follow up
3. If funding is available, hold a well-organized press briefing—this works better when there's a recent or upcoming news event to pique media interest
4. Stay on message—repetition is still the most effective means of penetration.

Dominating Opposition

The problem: Well-funded opposition is dominating how the issue is framed. They may be buttressing an effective news strategy with paid advertising. If an industry, they may be using traditional pro-business frames (i.e., anti-regulation, freedom, individualism, jobs, etc.) to good advantage.

Counter-strategies: Start by thoroughly researching your opposition. How are they funded? What are their real interests? What's at stake for them? Do they have front or "astroturf" organizations posing as grassroots groups or "concerned citizens"? Delegitimizing false claims and undermining their "moral" authority can be an effective strategy.

Sometimes, the problem is simply getting covered in the face of such high-profile media. This is the time to be creative. Develop innovative media events that can help draw attention to your issue. Some groups engage in street theater, youth-focused events or using non-traditional venues to get media attention. One group conducted a mock funeral in front of a target's home to dramatize a company's impact on the local environment.

Also important, but often ignored, are "alternative" media outlets. These weekly publications and magazines often do a more in-depth job of reporting and are more willing to take on vested interests than corporate-owned dailies. They are also widely read by local mainstream print and electronic media professionals in search of story ideas.

It is also important to re-evaluate your message: What symbols or shared values should your frame be evoking? Are there false claims or myths you should be countering directly? Who is best to deliver the counter-message? It is important to strike a balance between being reactive and being *responsive* to obstacles and opportunities as they develop.

Tough Customer

The problem: Every once in a while, you get a reporter or producer who is just plain hostile. They may have a personal relationship with the issue or a past beef with the organization that affects their ability to do fair reporting. (Of course, the vast majority of media professionals rise above their personal feelings and put their job first.)

Counter-strategies: The best strategy is to avoid the individual. Think creatively about reframing the story in ways that facilitate the cultivation of new relationships. For example, forego another pitch to a recalcitrant city desk editor and try a business or health reporter instead. In most cases, balanced coverage from other sources will reduce the impact of bias.

A Word About the Internet

This chapter has focused mostly on print and traditional broadcast media because currently, these are the mass media. Although the Internet is growing rapidly, the demographics are that its users are mainly white, young and mostly middle class. Without serious advocacy to guarantee access for the rest of us, organizers cannot depend on the Internet as the medium for reaching people at the grassroots level. Still, the Internet shows promise as an important communications tool in advocating policy. Campaigns to free jailed activist Mumia Abu Jamal and to win changes in the Telecommunications Act have effectively used the Internet to show support and spread the word.

Currently, advocacy groups use the Internet mostly to research issues or to communicate directly to members and supporters (i.e., to generate e-mail messages to policymakers, letters of protest, share information or to publicize events or actions). Some groups use real-time conferencing to hold low-cost, accessible meetings online. These meetings can be strategy sessions, information exchanges or trainings that, if participants have access to the Internet, will usually cost no more than a local phone call and their Internet access fees.

On-line versions of articles are usually different from the version that appears in print and, because of easy access, they are increasingly becoming the preferred sources for citation and research. Activists should take care to monitor electric versions of stories when possible. If the article is an in-depth one, background materials that do not appear in the print version may be posted online.

Websites are also another venue for getting the message out. A good website is crafted with the media and organizing strategy in mind. Its content should be consistent with organizational goals and should reinforce and amplify any campaign work the organization undertakes. For example, if a group is launching a policy initiative to expand funding for public transportation, its website should include background information on the initiative, how to get involved and some mechanism for sign-up. Added features like online registration cost money, but may be worth it if they can help build the volunteer base.

Some issues, like gun control and tobacco control, invite fierce opposition. Each group has to weigh the benefits of public access to their information online against opponent infiltration and monitoring. It makes sense not to leave much room for opponents to monitor an initiative's strategy and plans. Usually, striking a balance between good, supportive content and common-sense security measures provides adequate safeguards.

There is another reason for including the Internet in any media strategy: more and more, news media and policymakers are looking to electronic mail as an indication of public attitudes. For news media, people with computers are people with money and resources—prime targets for their advertisers. Policymakers online tend to pay more attention to e-mail input than to regular mail for much the same reason. Elected officials often respond to e-mail messages in half the time it takes to elicit a response via postal mail. Remember, any mass e-mail strategy must take place over a short period of time in order to have maximum impact.

Final Thoughts

To win the hearts and minds of people, forget the dry facts and statistics; tell them the stories that won you to the cause.

— FRED ROSS, SR., ORGANIZER, TEACHER AND COFOUNDER
OF THE UNITED FARM WORKERS UNION [18]

Media advocacy, at its best, effectively communicates a vision. That is when we stop *providing information* and begin *telling stories.* Stories are powerful and ancient things. They can evoke our deepest fears or connect us to our highest aspirations. And storytelling requires different skills than information dissemination. The data aren't as important as the images portraying why your issue is so compelling and important.

Currently, most of the stories told by the opposition fall into the "fear" category: fear of job loss, lowered property values, lack of personal safety, etc. It's a difficult frame to counter because it seems so real, so seductive, so palpable. On the other hand, public-interest work necessarily embodies a great deal of hope and faith. We must believe that policies and programs can make a difference. And we must believe in institutional accountability and the existence of a social contract. These are bedrock values that, regardless of our particular issue, guide our work.

Therefore, all activists working in the public interest share a common media goal: to counter the rhetoric of fear and isolation with that of institutional accountability and community-building. This common goal should guide the development of supportive, coordinated messages much like "the right" has developed coordinated messages on values of individualism and defunding programs, presumably because individuals and families—not programs—should provide support. Working together, we can create a louder, more sustained echo in the media to advance all public interest issues.

Anti-tobacco activists have already shown how such coordination can make a difference. These advocates took on a multi-billion dollar industry. It took money, research and hundreds of local coalitions wired together on one online service for almost a decade, but the results are phenomenal: tobacco companies have finally been forced to curb advertising and pay states billions of dollars to settle health claims. By using principles of institutional accountability to frame their issues, tobacco-control advocates were able to dramatically shift public discourse and policymaking in their favor.

Finally, as advocates we have to do a better job with our use of language. We use way too many words, we are too caught up in innovation and complexity, and we give up on our old words too easily once they come under attack. Instead of words like "sustainable environments," we might consider more accessible terms like "places where we can live well and be healthy." Instead of inventing new words to avoid the stigma of old ones—such as substituting "organizing" for "advocacy"— we might learn a lesson fom the right and be consistent with our language until we can turn perceptions around. After all, it wasn't long ago that "conservative" was a bad word and "welfare" a good one.

6

LOOKING AHEAD:

Reflections and Recommendations

> "Now, here, you see, it takes all the running you can do, to keep in the same place. If you want to get somewhere else, you must run at least twice as fast as that!"
>
> —THE QUEEN IN LEWIS CARROLL, *ALICE'S ADVENTURES IN WONDERLAND* [1]

Policy is an ever-changing, ever-evolving process. And nothing in public-interest policy, to paraphrase the ancient Greek philosopher Heraclitus, endures but change. Policies that were once on the cutting edge have been upstaged by succeeding ordinances they inspired. Usually, each policy improves upon the last because the greater the body of precedence, the bolder local jurisdictions become in pursuing the full range of legislative possibility.

Confronting the Opposition

Much of the success in the local policy arena has come from being undetected. The very limits of geography have kept local policy work below the radar of most opposing interests. As these movements gain a higher profile, exchange ideas and have more of an impact on powerful interests, opponents are taking note—and taking action. Affected companies are increasingly fighting back by inundating local governments and community-based agencies with attorneys pleading their cause, information requests and plain old-fashioned harassment tactics. These challenges threaten to stifle not only local policy work but the very foundations of democracy and free speech.

Addressing these challenges will require learning new skills and building new alliances as well as some substantial strengthening of old ones. One of the first things we must learn to do is abandon the slavish commitment to the separatism of discipline and category and begin to see our issue-oriented work as part of a whole movement for community healing and recovery. This does not mean we have to stop doing what we're doing or do more of what someone else is doing. It does mean that, if we want to truly become a "movement" for social justice, we must recognize that we are part of a vast division of labor with no one sector more important than the other. Our job is not to make everyone figure out how to get behind one issue. But we must learn how these issues (tobacco control, living wage, environmental justice, etc.) all connect and in doing so, at the very least, figure out how to build more synapses between our various cells.

UNDER THE MAGNIFYING GLASS

One way we can work together better is by sharing information and strategies for dealing with opposition. A successful example of such collaboration is found in the effort to fight changes in the laws governing nonprofit tax-exempt status and advocacy.

Coalitions engaged in policy work are under extra scrutiny by both public and private funders as a direct result of industry pressure on funders about their grantees. Funded coalitions working in tobacco control, drug prevention, youth development and violence prevention have experienced dramatic—and negative—changes in grant procedures as a direct result of their policy work. Federal agencies providing this funding have been singled out for industry pressure.

The federal Center for Substance Abuse Prevention (CSAP), which funds advocacy groups, was the target of a General Accounting Office investigation, congressional hearings and budget cuts in the space of one year—all led by the National Beer Wholesalers Association (NBWA), which openly bragged in trade publications and in other media that its goal was to open a "multifront war" on the agency.[2]

NBWA built a coalition of like-minded business interests that wanted to hit agencies where they hurt most: their budgets. It was quickly joined by other conservative groups, including the Cato Institute, the John Locke Foundation and the Christian Coalition. Together, they pushed for far-ranging legislation in 1995 to revise federal tax laws and spending policies so that policy advocacy by nonprofit groups would be severely restricted. The bill, known as the Istook

Amendment, also provided for the complete dismantling of CSAP. Said NBWA lobbyist, David Rehr:

> It drives our wholesalers nuts to know that their tax dollars are being used by groups that are trying to drive them out of business. This is our response: We want to cut off their funding, stop their lobbying and basically end the use of that structure to bash the beer industry.[3]

When the bill passed out of its House subcommittee, Coors Brewing Company thanked committee members with a gift of two cases of beer. NBWA sent six-packs of beer to every supporter on Capitol Hill. NBWA also invested a great deal of resources into organizing its members. It sent out 7,000 faxes and dedicated five full-time staff to pushing the legislation. Their efforts greatly impressed Congressman Ernest Istook, who sponsored the amendment, moving him to remark, "I don't know any group that lobbied as hard as the beer wholesalers."[4]

Fortunately, a strong national coalition of nonprofit groups kept the bill from being voted into law, but it's sure not to be business's last attempt to stop policy advocacy by nonprofit groups. In some ways, the mere introduction of the bill has accomplished the desired chilling effect: CSAP has greatly restricted the policy advocacy work of its grantees. And another federally funded program, the ASSIST Project (a tobacco-control initiative of the National Cancer Institute), issued several procedural changes to restrict grantees' policy activities during 1995. At one point, ASSIST was so concerned about outside pressure from tobacco-industry interest concerning its grantees' policy work that staff held up written materials for an advocacy training for nonprofit groups at its October 1995 national meeting until they were sure that no legislative work would be discussed.[5]

Nongovernmental funders are also cracking down on advocacy groups pursuing local legislative work, even though that work is within the limits of the law. The mixed signals and cautiousness from funders have created confusion among grantees, who are pulled between the limitations of their funding and the needs of their community. A national anti-drug initiative receiving private foundation support, for example, reports that their funder requested that the words "policy" and "advocacy" be removed from any initiative materials—even the materials not funded by the foundation. "[The foundation] kept telling me they wanted to be extra careful because of issues raised by [their] board members," said a member of the group.[6]

The people who work for nonprofit organizations have the same rights to free speech and assembly as anyone else in this country, but you would never know that from listening to some policymakers. A strange logic prevails when it comes to the participation of nonprofits in governance. As outlined in the laws governing their nonprofit IRS status, groups with nonprofit tax status are not allowed to take a position on pertinent public policy issues because they receive public funding and, ostensibly, the subsidy of tax-exempt status. Corporations, on the other hand, also receive public dollars (much more in fact) plus a whole range of tax subsidies, including those associated with corporate status; but somehow they are different in the eyes of the law and are not subjected to such restrictions. Both are important sectors of the economy and both create jobs.

Advocates, by their very expertise, should be in the center of the public policy process—not shut out from it. If tobacco-control advocates, for example, cannot offer their educated perspective on tobacco control, only the tobacco industry can participate in the discussion. The same is true for advocates working on health care, guns, child welfare and more. If the organizations that are formed to study and work on these issues cannot fully participate in the legislative process, that process is abandoned to the control of for-profit interests.

Creating this monopoly, as the case of the beer wholesalers illustrates, is precisely the goal of legislation to silence advocacy groups. Rather than asking organizations to adapt to these increasingly draconian rules, funders and policymakers should support the development of coordinated strategies to fight back. New laws should be introduced to expand the participation of nonprofits in the public policy process, not limit it. And organizations should consider pushing closer to the boundaries of the IRS rules about lobbying and even test them with carefully crafted legal challenges when appropriate. Moreover, this double standard must end. Any laws restricting lobbying should be applied across the board to every institutional recipient of public funding.

Unfortunately, recent trends in Congress promise otherwise. A 1998 law passed as a one-sentence rider on a 4,000-page federal appropriations bill guarantees corporations access to the raw data and related notes of publicly funded *nonprofit* research through the Freedom of Information Act (FOIA). The author of the policy, Alabama Senator Richard Shelby, says that the law will provide "taxpayers" with access to the research their money has paid for. Scientists, activists and academicians see the law (which passed without public hearings or comment) as a way to hamper controversial research projects and thwart regulatory activity. Corporate research was excluded from the law. Only nonprofit organizations, including universities, are affected.

Given industry's steady, costly and disruptive FOIA activity with regard to advocacy initiatives, this law is sure to make things worse—especially since business interests have made the law and its implementation a high priority. The United States Chamber of Commerce provides one example of the keen business interest in the law in this excerpt from its web site: "In the regulatory reform arena there may never be a more important issue....If implemented properly, this rule will do more for regulatory reform than all the legislation passed in the last 10 years!"[7]

PREEMPTIVE STRIKE

In addition to threatening nonprofits' funding, opponents are working to undermine the legal framework of local control that makes many of the policy initiatives advanced by community activists possible. Local jurisdictions, cities and county governments have certain powers that are usually out of the reach of state and federal lawmakers. Land use and planning, which includes zoning, are among the tools of local governance that have recently come under attack. The opposition's technique is to enact a state or federal law that would preempt, or make invalid, a local one. Fair housing, alcohol policy, tobacco control and gun control are among the policy arenas where industry interests are pushing state and federal legislation to preempt local laws.

Opponents claim they need such preemption because the "patchwork" of local laws makes it difficult for them to do business. They say they need limited regulation that is consistent on at least a statewide basis. The real story may be that opponents know that grassroots efforts would have a much harder time affecting state and federal governments. It requires more votes and a more varied support base. Local initiatives are, more often than not, enacted in urban areas to address specific problems. Trying to make the case for such initiatives at the state level can be difficult—especially to the increasing number of legislators representing districts without urban centers.

Unfortunately, due to census undercounting, low voter turnout and other barriers, urban interests are often not adequately represented at the state level and suburban-based officials often comprise a legislature's majority. Also, local activists rarely have the means to adequately monitor state legislative activity, while their opponents usually employ full-time lobbyists. All of this has added up to a slew of preemption initiatives that have caused a significant drain on the resources and attention of local activists.

Fighting preemption will take a coordinated strategy that cuts across the various issues activists are working on to address the fundamental principle of local control. Of course, local control is not a panacea, as there is a wide range of social problems that local policy alone can never address. However, local jurisdictions should be allowed to provide residents with as many protections and benefits as possible and these protections should be augmented, not limited, by state and federal legislation.

We need to develop model state and federal anti-preemption legislation that cuts across a variety of issues and articulates a standard for lawmaking that is supportive of local control while enabling state or federal legislative bodies to continue to set minimum standards or intervene when necessary. For example, such legislation would allow local jurisdictions to develop more stringent air quality regulations than state and/or federal standards while setting minimum controls so that every community is protected to some degree.

Too often, preemption legislation is designed to hold local governments hostage to the most minimum levels of regulatory activity, in the purported interest of cutting red tape and providing a consistent business climate. More research is needed, however, to test these assumptions. Related studies in the area of business regulation suggest that businesses thrive in communities that set standards for their operations. This is true mainly because a good business climate is not determined by the absence of regulation, but by the presence of well-functioning social infrastructures like public schools, roads, quality housing and the like. Good infrastructures require good stewardship of local resources, of which conscientious policymaking is a critical part.

LAWSUITS AND OTHER LEGAL MANEUVERS

Another common tactic of opponents is to threaten local jurisdictions with lawsuits. The goal of these threats is to intimidate local public officials and residents with the prospect of an expensive civil action. Richmond, California's 1992 Measure J Campaign offers a case in point. The measure to restrict alcohol and tobacco billboard advertising from within 2,000 feet of schools and day care centers qualified for the city ballot with overwhelming support. To fight it, the billboard industry invested hundreds of thousands of dollars in ads featuring this straight-forward threat: "Does Richmond Have $500,000 to Burn?"

The ads were clear that if Richmond residents passed the measure, the industry would sue the city for at least that amount. Richmond is not an affluent city. At the time, Richmond schools were in receivership and the city faced the prospect of a budget deficit; residents feared more financial hardship. Still, even under threat of bankruptcy, the measure only failed by a four percent margin. Yet opponents had outspent supporters 500 to 1.[8]

Industry lawsuits are more than idle threats. They are common real-life occurrences. Virtually every local policy that has been enacted to regulate billboard advertising has been litigated in court. Tobacco control, alcohol policy, gun control and environmental justice are other areas of policymaking being attacked by lawsuits. It doesn't seem to matter how benign the policy may be, if it can encourage other jurisdictions to pass a law, then opponents seem ready to block its implementation.

An extreme example of this phenomenon comes from Texas, where groups affiliated with the National Rifle Association were unhappy with a 1996 state law that restricted carrying concealed weapons in a few places, including churches and hospitals. The groups wanted the right to pack their pistols anywhere, including where they worship. So, they took legal action to have all of the exceptions removed from the law—and won.

One promising trend is the increased interest of attorneys and associations of lawyers in providing pro bono (free) legal services to defend voter-passed initiatives. Organizations like the National Lawyers Guild, the National Conference of Black Lawyers and the Mexican American Legal Defense and Education Fund are providing lawyers, technical assistance and, occasionally, funding to organizations embroiled in these lawsuits. Thanks to the Internet, groups are sharing legal strategies, briefs and research on the opposition, which help these organizations defend policies more effectively.

Another exciting development is the growing proliferation of resource centers designed to provide legal support and assistance to activists working on specific issues. These include the Tobacco Product Liabilities Project, which serves tobacco control activists, and the Environmental Justice Resource Center, Tulane Environmental Law Center and the long-standing NAACP Legal Defense and Education

Fund, which serve the environmental justice movement and activists working in civil rights. It is hoped that multi-issue centers like the University of Denver's Political Litigation Project will also expand, as a broad multi-issue approach to these legal initiatives is certainly needed.

Funders need to expand their support for these centers to meet the growing demand for services. Too many groups in desperate need of legal help are turned away each year. In addition, funders should help create more venues where activists and the legal workers who support them can meet and discuss emerging issues. Advocacy groups and lawyers who "represent" the public interest have particular issues to work through, including how to collaborate across different professional cultures, and how to share power and expertise. A recent, public struggle between the Los Angeles Bus Riders Union and its attorneys over the direction of a class action suit only underscores the need for more discussion—and debate—on the role of legal work in advocacy and social change.[9]

It is also important to note that legal *defense* should not be the only strategy employed to fight litigation by opponents. In addition to responding to lawsuits to push public and private institutions, activists should consider working for public policies that would reduce the use of what are known as Strategic Lawsuits Against Public Participation (or SLAPPs). Thanks to activist work, a number of states have enacted laws restricting the use of SLAPPs. These protections should be expanded. Working together, lawyers and activists can advance these and other strategies to advocate for public policy.

Addressing Issues of Gender and Race

Media pundits have dubbed this period the era of "angry white men." We are told they are angry about affirmative action, gay rights, women's rights, the economy and more. They long for the "good old days" when they were on top and the living was easy. Although it's not clear that there ever were any "good old days" outside of these angry guys' imagination, it is certain that there is a backlash against basic human rights for women, people of color and other traditionally disfranchised people.

Hard-won reforms by the women's movement, including access to birth control and equal access to public funding and resources (such as Title IX requirements for the support of women athletes) are under attack. Civil rights victories, including voting rights policy, fair housing and school equity laws have an even more tenuous future. Affirmative action has been hardest hit, with the right virtually reframing it as "quotas for the unqualified" instead of a tool for recruitment and retrofitting for diversity.

Proponents for dismantling these policies claim that they are working to develop a policy framework that is more fair and neutral than the civil rights framework. Yet they use negative and demeaning stereotypes like "welfare queens" and "feminazis" (meaning feminism equals fascism) to build support for their essentially anti-human policies. It could well be that their intent is honorable. However, as social change agents, *we must not be concerned with intent but with outcomes.* Our job is to make sure that the *results* of any policy bring us closer to equity and justice regardless of its intentions.

Therefore, we must pay attention to the role of racism, sexism and other forms of oppression in the framing and implementation of policies. Given the importance of equity (equal access to services, jobs, transportation, education, etc.) in human development and well being, policies must not just be race- and gender-*neutral*, they must whenever possible create opportunities and address inequity or, in other words, be race- and gender-*positive*. Unfortunately, given the fact that much of recent federal policymaking is race- and gender-*negative*, aggressive counterstrategies are needed to turn this trend around.

The welfare reform enacted in 1997 provides a potent example of how negatively "gendered" and "racialized" discourse helped to create policy that is similarly negative in the way it affects people by gender and race. This massive social policy was advanced with three basic beliefs at its foundation. First, that parenting was not work: these recipients—women at home with children—were not "working" but just sitting around getting a check. Second, that most of these women were black and Latino and, given prevailing stereotypes, were therefore at a *cultural* disadvantage in that they purportedly did not understand the mechanics or value of work. And third, that these women would fare much better in the marketplace than in a publicly funded social service structure (i.e., private is better).

Many organizers fighting welfare reform focused mainly on the lack of available jobs, childcare and transportation for women in transition to "self sufficiency" (meaning employment). There was little discussion of the gender implications of concepts like "work" or "self sufficiency" or the racial implications of concepts like "culture of poverty." Further, welfare reform is completely dependent on the labor market, but there was little effort to build in any protections against employment discrimination based on gender and race. Given the high numbers of women and people of color who are transitioning into the labor market and the common occurrence of discrimination, it would seem plausible that such protections should be strengthened. In fact, recent news coverage that whites are finding jobs faster than blacks and Latinos only reinforces the need for such protections. [10] However, awareness of racism and sexism are not as much a part of the public discourse as are stories about how racism and sexism are insignificant—especially when compared to individual and cultural attributes. Policy has just followed suit.

IT'S (STILL) A MAN'S WORLD

As Susan Faludi so powerfully documents in her book *Backlash*, dismantling the gains of the women's movement has been at the center of the conservative agenda. And the results of these attacks are more than mere changes in custom. [11]

Women and girls are facing a crisis of huge proportions. Among the many challenges facing them are credit discrimination, policies mandating that agencies disclose the sexual activity of clients who are female minors, and the lack of funding for women's health issues. Few policies address the institutionalized framework of patriarchy in public policy; recent trends in policymaking promise to expand gender inequities.

State and federal policies to address teen pregnancy, for example, have increasingly focused on controlling the bodies of young women by making sterilization, contraceptive implants, or limiting the number of children as a condition of receiving entitlements. These are some of the repressive policies and policy proposals aimed at young women and poor families. Further, teen girls, who run away most often because of abuse in the home, are in most states required to stay with their parent or lose benefits. In short, the insertion of "family values" in the policy arena has meant devaluing women and girls.

Fortunately, there are women's groups that are fighting back and, more important, organizing young women and girls to advance a gender-positive agenda to address institutional sexism in the U.S. and internationally. One area where public health, institutional sexism and public policy have positively intersected is in the prevention of domestic violence.

When those advocating the prevention of domestic violence

reviewed the federal welfare reform legislation, they were concerned that the bill did not provide adequate protections for the many women who were in transition from battering relationships. There were already women who stayed in battering relationships so that they (and often, their children) could have enough income to live on. Public benefits helped to provide some measure of self-sufficiency for women who wanted to leave such relationships until they could heal and prepare for new lives.

Nationally, domestic violence prevention groups prevailed upon Congress and the President to include clauses encouraging states to suspend benefit time limits for recipients who were victims of domestic violence. Thanks to their efforts, the bill was amended to enable states to make allowances for battering victims. Still, advocates had to work on a state-by-state basis to ensure effective implementation of these allowances. Most states did implement special protections for battering victims under the watchful eye of women-led coalitions—many of which were funded through state and private foundation partnerships.

There are many other issues to tackle, especially in public health. Prevention and treatment programs for women and girls are woefully underfunded. States and local health service departments could craft budgets that would guarantee that an appropriate percentage of funding was set aside for women and girls. There are numerous models to choose from, including the Women's Budget of the Women's International League for Peace and Freedom. [12]

Access to contraceptives and other forms of reproductive health care is another important issue. Young women in inner-city communities are rarely given alternatives beyond the invasive measures of sterilization and long-term birth control implants lasting several years, often with harsh side effects. Many of these young women have no access to health care at all and will risk pregnancy instead. San Francisco's Youth Making A Change (see Chapter 4) provides a dynamic model for expanding youth access to care. These young people are leading a fight to get their mayor to fund more clinics in high schools rather than more police. Before the campaign, only one high school in San Francisco had a clinic. As of this writing, the group has won funding for an additional clinic and continues to fight for five more—one for each high school. [13]

As chain stores take over rural and small town markets, women living in these areas also face shrinking health care options. Wal-Mart stores, for example, are under pressure by women's groups for refusing to carry Preven, a post-coital or "morning after" pill most commonly used after rape or incest. Besides Preven, which is legal in the U.S., many other contraceptive choices available in Europe and other parts of the world are banned by the federal government.[14] These public and private reproductive health policies have a tremendous impact on women's health that must be understood and articulated, expanding the issues beyond the pro-choice or anti-abortion rights discussion. Activists can craft and advance policies at both the state and local health department level that help to expand reproductive health care and, unlike the opposition, our policies should take into account women's sexual realities and needs for both safety and pleasure.

There are many more gender-related issues that require attention and tenacity. And there are organizations that are dealing specifically with sexism and gender oppression as part of their policy work. But there should be many more and this work should not be limited to "women's groups." Every group should examine the gender aspects of social issues and be willing to develop initiatives that seek to address this important injustice as well.

THE INCREASING SIGNIFICANCE OF RACE

Policy work is becoming increasingly "racialized," meaning that race and racism are now prominent features of virtually any discourse in public policy.

It makes sense that so much policy work would involve race relations. Racism is a system that has engendered a myriad of institutions and infrastructures to sustain it: ghettoes and suburbs, public school inequities, biased standardized testing, unequal access to public transportation, redlining—the list goes on. Local activists seeking policies to address fundamental causes of death, disease and injustice must address the structural nature of racism. This requires an awareness of how these factors shape public policy and public life.

Interestingly enough, activists who tackle the race issue head-on are often accused by their peers and opponents alike of being divisive or engaging in less important "identity politics" instead of addressing the real issue at hand. Yet, opponents are increasingly relying on coded language about race to build support for a number of policy initiatives.

One way to check for racial coding: if the discussion has divided those affected by a policy into "we" and "they," chances are that a light scratch of the surface will reveal racial tensions underneath. Welfare reform, immigration restrictions and the so-called War on Drugs are just

a few examples of how opponents are exploiting racism, fear and big-
otry to justify policies that shift public monies from social services to law
enforcement. Terms like "crackhead," "welfare queen," and "super-
predator" have for years been loaded with racial imagery of the worst
possible kind. More recent discussions on immigration focus on controlling U.S. borders to the south. Fears of dark people taking over the
country translate into a slew of policies proposed to cut support and
protections for low-wage earners from countries whose depressed
economies are often the result of U.S. policies.

Activists cannot back away from this conversation on race and
hope to win in the public policy arena—particularly in electoral contests. It is difficult to win any game with just defense. When race comes
into play, if activists' only strategy is to attempt to refute stereotypes and
hope for the best, then the game is already lost. The most successful
strategy is to get on the offensive, identify any elements of a policy initiative that would disproportionately harm disfranchised communities
(racial, ethnic or otherwise) and raise the unfairness directly, utilizing
available civil rights protections.

In fact, race is such an important construct for understanding policy that activists should be initiating its consideration in policymaking,
not ignoring it. One great example of such initiative comes from the
environmental justice movement. Activists from communities of color
have coined the phrase *environmental racism* to refer to targeting communities of color for environmentally compromising uses and the
phrase *environmental justice* to refer to remedies to address this targeting.
These terms have served to reframe and redefine an entire movement
that was ignoring the racial implications of environmental policies.

Prior to the injection of race and justice into the environmental
policy discourse, "mainstream" activists mostly framed environmental
issues in relatively non-racial terms. Environmental justice activists had
to wage a debate both within the environmental movement and outside
of it in order to be heard. There were those in mainstream leadership
that accused these activists of being divisive but, although there are still
tensions, environmental justice work has helped invigorate environmental policy as a whole. It has yielded some of the movement's greatest victories and best media coverage. Most important, it has catalyzed
changes in law and institutional practice that directly address justice and
fair play.

By abdicating the debate on race to their opponents, activists also
abdicate a leadership role in defining the underlying issue that's so

much a part of these discussions: the terms and obligations of the social contract. By working for the defunding of programs and initiatives designed to address the needs of those who are, historically, disfranchised and oppressed, opponents are also rewriting the social contract (or set of obligations) that, until now, has operated on the belief that government should use resources to improve the quality of life and create equal opportunities for all who live in this country. Ignoring these fundamental shifts in the role of government has paved the way for other "revisions" in the contract, including government abandonment of its role as business "watchdog," which has resulted in deregulation in numerous sectors of business.

Truly addressing issues of racism in policy will require new data sets and new approaches to research and advocacy that take these issues head-on. First, more research must disaggregate its findings by race and ethnicity. Class (income) and gender are also important to identify, as these factors can illuminate important trends and patterns, but not enough studies sensitively deal with racial impact. In fact, much of the work that views social problems exclusively through the lens of class tends to obscure the role of racism.

Second, activists must count the fact that opponents are increasingly turning to the electoral arena to push through anti-health and anti-community initiatives. The pool of regular voters has shrunk to a small elite of mostly white, middle-class voters. By appealing to the most negative and narrow interests of this group, opponents have leveraged fear and ignorance into victories at the polls. Anti-affirmative-action measures have been successful when voters believe stories of "unqualified" people of color "stealing" jobs or college placements from "more qualified" whites. Laws mandating life imprisonment have passed when voters believe stories of released murderers who left prison only to kill again. While these stories do not reflect the whole picture, they are effective in moving this small segment of voters that do show up (about 30 percent of registered voters nationally) to cast their ballots.

Few organizations or political parties are registering people in communities of color, much less developing systems for regular voter tracking and getting people out to vote. Yet, with the low turnout in most electoral contests, a directed voter strategy in these communities could make a real difference in key states and cities nationwide. Groups like Californians for Justice (CFJ) are proving that activists who work to build electoral power through old-fashioned precinct organizing and voter turnout drives can have an impact on these initiatives and even mount a few of their own. In just two years, CFJ increased voter registration and participation in traditionally low-income communities and communities of color in California. Because of this added power at the polls, CFJ precincts support progressive initiatives (and oppose regressive ones) in higher numbers than other, even demographically similar, California precincts and they have consistently won the vote where they did out-reach. Of course, with more resources they could reach even more people.

Third, we have to learn new ways of working together. Racism is like the gorilla in the living room. It's running through the place mak-ing noises and everyone is trying to sit politely and ignore it. There are privileges and pain associated with racism that are often too loaded for us to deal with, but it's most important to remember that first and fore-most, racism is a system that is much larger than the sum of the indi-viduals who are affected by it. In order to address racism effectively, we have to de-personalize it, understand its systemic nature and not take personally the inevitable culture and power clashes that occur as we learn how to build new, less comfortable alliances.

Whites can and must play a constructive role in this debate. A 1997 local initiative to repeal affirmative action in Houston (Proposition A) provides a great model. Unlike most places where such an initiative has been launched, it was defeated in Houston. This success was large-ly due to a media campaign featuring the city's outspoken, white mayor, Bob Lanier. Among the mayor's oft-repeated sound bites in the defense of affirmative action was the following:

> Anglo male contractors got between 95 percent and 99 percent of the [city's] business before the affirmative action program got started about 12 years ago. Today they still get 80 percent. They want more. That's the bottom line.

Analysis by the Berkeley Media Studies Group concluded that that kind of honest, direct message from the highest levels about institu-tionalized racism was critical to Proposition A's defeat.[15]

Retrofitting for Battle

Building a *movement* requires, at the very least, a sense of collec-tivity, processes of communication, shared values, and a broad common purpose. And we need a movement to address the attacks against poor and low-wage-earning people that are coming from all sides. And yes, they are attacks, and whether we are willing to shoot back or merely run for cover, we are in the middle of a war.

The more we face this fact, the better prepared we'll be to deal with its implications. Funders will stop asking us to invite those with opposing interests to sit at our strategy table. We'll invest in building the capacity to fight for good policies and not simply to educate the community with yet another program. Not that programs aren't important, but one would not go to battle and only set up hospitals and recreation centers. Soldiers and weapons are also needed to forge new covenants and win new victories.

Retrofitting for battle will require better communication among allies working on various issues and at various levels of change. Funders are in a particularly important position to make this happen by developing networks of grantees that can at least lay a rudimentary foundation for such an infrastructure. It will also mean better coordination of media objectives. If we have learned nothing else from the right, it is that coordinated media coverage across a variety of issues can work to advance our purpose. If their message is personal responsibility and scapegoating, then ours must be institutional change and the social contract.

By developing networks that include activists, researchers and intermediary organizations, funders can provide the critical venue for the development of shared language, strategies and vision. The new electronic media, if we can expand public access to them, offer incredible opportunities for creating such venues. Taking advantage of these opportunities will require capacity building, investment in organizational infrastructure and advocacy to ensure community access to this technology. Tobacco-control efforts have already proven the success of these methods.

The Future Looks Bright

> Our awesome responsibility to ourselves, to our children, and to our
> future is to create ourselves in the image of goodness, because the
> future depends on the nobility of our imaginings.
>
> —BARBARA GRIZZUTI HARRISON

Perhaps the most striking lesson for me in more than a decade of doing this work is the extent to which so many people of so many backgrounds share a common dream of community. Through leading trainings, I've had the chance to have small-group, intensive interaction with about 10,000 people. Often, we ask participants to draw pictures of their ideal world. It doesn't matter what race they are or how much money they have, whether they came in a Lexus or they came in a bus—their pictures look much the same. The world is green. Their communities are circular. They are villages with few cars and lots of space.

It has always been a small miracle to me to see how concrete this vision remains for so many people. Yet, what distinguishes the artists in large part is the sense of the *possibility* of achieving this vision. Some are worried about questions such as: Do the "other people" deserve this, too? Are they capable of handling it? If everybody has access to this can I get or keep mine? Theirs is an analysis based on their perceptions of individuals' weaknesses.

Interestingly enough, there are those who focus on the role of institutions in maintaining the decidedly less-than-ideal status quo. They see corporate and government policy as part of an institutional network of inequity and that analysis frames their perspective. And of course, there are many, many people who lie some where in between.

Our politics and beliefs about the world are, therefore, not shaped by different *visions* of the ideal, but by different beliefs about the possibility of achieving this ideal. Perhaps that is why people tend to relegate idealism to the more halcyon days of youth.

Our job as activists is to demonstrate the possibility of realizing this ideal, to articulate this "hidden transcript," or popular imagination, in ways that allow people to recognize it as their own. Local policy work has the potential for such incremental, yet fundamental, change—as long as it is seen as just that—incremental. It will require paying as much attention to the destination as we pay to the journey, but by working one step at a time, one policy at a time, our collective work can build hope and belief in the noblest of our imaginings.

Notes

INTRODUCTION

1. E. Johnson. Interview, June 20, 1994.

2. National Institutes of Health; National Cancer Institute. *Major Local Tobacco Control Ordinances in the United States.* Smoking and Tobacco Control Monograph No. 3. National Cancer Institute, Bethesda, MD, 1993.

3. Mark Pertschuk, Executive Director of Californians for Responsible Gun Laws. Interview, April 24, 1998.

4. See the New Party's Web Site, <www.newparty.org>, for information on living-wage campaigns.

5. T. S. Eliot. "La Figlia Che Piange," in *Complete Poems and Plays.* Harcourt-Brace, 1952, p. 20.

6. See N. S. Mayer. *Neighborhood Organizations and Community Development.* Urban Institute Press, Washington, D. C., 1984; and L. A. Curtis. "Policies to Prevent Crime: Neighborhood, family and employment strategies," *Annals of the American Academy of Political and Social Sciences,* 494:9+. 1987.

7. See D. W. McMillan, and D. M. Chavis. "Sense of community: A definition and theory," *Journal of Community Psychology,* 14:6–23. 1986.

8. See J. D. Hawkins, R. F. Catalano, and J. Y. Miller. "Risk and Protective Factors for Alcohol and Other Drug Problems in Adolescence and Early Adulthood: Implications for Substance Abuse Prevention," *Psychological Bulletin,* 112:64–105. 1992.

9. Carol Weiss, ed. *Organizations for Policy Analysis: Helping Government Think.* Sage Publications, 1992.

10. Ibid.

11. C. King, R. G. Robinson, and A. Ellis. "HARYOU-ACT and Black Youth in Rebellion," *Wilson Library Bulletin,* H. Wilson Publications, New York, October, 1967.

12. Joint Center for Political Studies. *Black Elected Officials: A National Roster 1986.* Unipub Publications, New York, 1986; and *Statistical Record of Black America*, Third Edition. Gale Publishers, Detroit, MI, 1994.

13. Ibid.

CHAPTER 1

1. D. Beauchamp. "Public Health as Social Justice," *Inquiry*. 12:3–14. 1976.

2. Holly Sklar. *Chaos or Community? Seeking Solutions, Not Scapegoats for Bad Economics*. South End Press, 1995, p. 26.

3. David Korten. *When Corporations Rule the World*. Kumarian Press, West Hartford, CT, 1995.

4. Sklar, p. 10.

5. Korten, p. 226.

6. Sklar, p. 32.

7. D. P. Rice, S. Kelman, L. S. Miller, S. Dunmeyer. *The Economic Costs of Alcohol and Drug Abuse and Mental Illness: 1985,* Institute for Health and Aging, University of California, San Francisco, CA, 1990. (Figures cited are calculated from data in the study.)

8. J. M. McKnight. "Health in the Post Medical Era," *Health and Medicine,* Winter, 4, 1982, p. 4.

9. Quoted in William Leach. *Land of Desire: Merchants, Power and the Rise of a New American Culture*. Vintage Books, 1993, p. 298.

10. Robert Heilbroner.*The Nature and Logic of Capitalism*. W.W. Norton & Company, New York, 1986, p. 36.

11. Leach, op. cit.

12. Leach, p. 10.

13. D. Fleming. "Total U. S. drinks volumes are flat, but growth is strong in key areas," *Impact International* 13(14/15): 1–4. August 1 & 15, 1998.

14. See Lawrence Wallack, Joel Grube, Patricia Madden, Warren Breed. "Portrayals of alcohol on prime-time television," *Journal of Studies on Alcohol*, 51(5), 1990; Joel Grube. "Alcohol portrayals and alcohol advertising on television: content and effects on children and adolescents," *Alcohol Health & Research World*, 17(1), 1993; Joel Grube and Lawrence Wallack. "Television beer advertising and drinking knowledge, beliefs, and intentions among schoolchildren," *American Journal of Public Health*, 84(2), February, 1994; and Lawrence Wallack, Diana Cassady, Joel Grube. *TV beer commercials and children: exposure, attention, beliefs, and expectations about drinking as an adult*, AAA Foundation for Traffic Safety, Washington, D. C., 1990.

15. Quoted in D. Belton, ed. *Speak My Name: Black Men on Masculinity and the American Dream*. Beacon Press, Boston, 1995.

16. James Scott. *Domination and the Arts of Resistance: Hidden Transcripts*. Yale University Press, 1990, page 223.

17. Scott, page 2.

CHAPTER 2

1. The Coup. "Big Cats, Bigga Fish," on *Genocide and Juice*, Wild Pitch Records, lyrics by R. Riley and E. Davis, 1994.

2. Jerry Thomas. "2nd malt liquor cited by protester," *Chicago Tribune*, August 22, 1991.

3. See D. Beauchamp. "Public Health as Social Justice," *Inquiry*. 12:3–14. 1976; and D. Massey. "American apartheid: Segregation and the making of the underclass," *Poverty and Race*, September 1, 1992, p.1.

4. J. F. Mosher. "Alcohol and Poverty: Analyzing the Link between Alcohol-Related Problems and Social Policy," in S. E. Samuels and M. D. Smith, eds. *Improving the Health of the Poor*. The Henry J. Kaiser Family Foundation, Menlo Park, CA, 1992.

5. See Mosher, ibid; also see J. Robow, and R. K. Watts. "Alcohol availability, alcohol beverage sales and alcohol-related problems," *Journal of Studies on Alcohol*, 43:767; 801. 1982.

6. R. G. Robinson, C. Sutton, M. Pertschuk. "Smoking and African Americans: Spotlighting the Effects of Smoking and Tobacco Promotion in the African American Community," in S. E. Samuels and M. D. Smith, eds. *Improving the Health of the Poor*. The Henry J. Kaiser Family Foundation, Menlo Park, CA, 1992.

7. See M. N. Themba, and R. G. Robinson. *Crossing Substances for Common Interest: An Examination of the Movement Against Targeted Alcohol and Tobacco Marketing and Its Implications for Public Health Coalitions*. Center for Substance Abuse Prevention, Rockville, MD, 1998.

8. Sylvia Castillo. Interview, April 5, 1998.

9. Calculated from historical data from the City of Los Angeles Planning Commission on types of businesses and business licenses from 1958 to 1970 in the 8th and 9th councilmanic districts—the two districts that make up most of what is considered South Central Los Angeles.

10. R. A. Scribner. *The Overconcentration Loophole*. USC School of Medicine, Local Alcohol Availability Database, 1992, p. 1.

11. J. F. Mosher, and R. M. Works. *Confronting Sacramento: State Preemption, Community Control, and Alcohol-Outlet Blight in Two Inner City Communities*. The Marin Institute, San Rafael, CA, 1994.

12. Mosher, "Alcohol and Poverty," p. 1.

13. Castillo, see note 8 above.

14. Mosher and Works, p. 18.

15. Castillo, see note 8 above.

16. Mosher and Works, p. 18.

17. Clarence Lusane. *African Americans at the Crossroads: The Restructuring of Black Leadership and the 1992 Elections*. South End Press, 1994, p.105.

18. J. T. Barrett. "Retailers and Restaurants Hard Hit By L. A. Riots," *Impact*, June 15, 1992.

19. Lusane, op. cit.

20. Mosher and Works, op. cit.

21. Mosher and Works, op. cit.

22. Castillo, see note 8 above.

23. Castillo.

24. Castillo.

25. Castillo.

26. Mosher and Works, op. cit

27. Castillo.

28. Kevin Jordan. Interview, January 21, 1994.

29. Jordan.

30. Mary Lou Kline, Interview, April 19, 1994.

31. Kline

32. Kline.

33. Jordan, see note 28.

34. Bev Thomas. Interview, January 5, 1994.

35. J. Jacobson. "High-powered lobby threatens bill to ban liquor advertising on billboards," *The Baltimore Sun*, April 2, 1993.

36. Thomas, see note 34 above.

37. *Maryland Report* [newspaper], May 17, 1993.

38. Ibid.

39. T. Bowman. "Billboard control bill is signed: Baltimore allowed to ban liquor ads on outdoor sites," *The Baltimore Sun*, May 28, 1993.

40. Christopher Fritz. Interview, April 20, 1994.

41. Fritz.

42. Thomas, see note 34 above.

43. Rev. Norman Handy. Interview, March 3, 1994.

44. "Protest and press conference scheduled," *The Baltimore Times*, December 6, 1993.

45. Ibid.

46. Jordan, see note 28 above.

47. Thomas, see note 34 above.

48. "Urban League wants to modify billboard ban," *The Baltimore Times*, October 25, 1993.

49. Ibid.

50. G. W. Collins. "Liquor lobbyists, billboard opponents prepare for bill-board clash," *The Baltimore Times*, November 1, 1993.

51. Thomas, see note 34 above.

52. Matthews Wright. Interview, March 11, 1994.

53. Jordan, see note 28 above.

54. J. Daemmrich. "Sign owners will cover 111 ads," *The Baltimore Sun*, November 5, 1993.

55. Thomas, see note 34 above.

56. Daemmrich, op. cit.

57. Thomas, see note 34 above.

58. See M. L. Alaniz, C. Wilkes. "Reinventing Culture. Reinterpreting Latino Culture in the Commodity Form: the case of alcohol advertising in the Mexican American community," *Hispanic Journal of Behavioral Sciences*, 17:4 (1995); M. L. Alaniz. "Gender Differences in Social Drinking Context and Networks Among Mexican American Husbands and Wives," *Addiction Research*, under review; and M. L. Alaniz and C. Wilkes. *Pro-drinking messages and message environment for Young Adults: The case of alcohol industry in African American, Mexican American, and Native American Communities*, Addiction Research Foundation, Toronto, Canada.

CHAPTER 3

1. Franklin Roosevelt. "Second Inaugural Address," January 20, 1937.

2. Calculated from 1996 Bureau of Labor Statistics. "Total Non-Farm Payroll and Total Government Payroll Annually Adjusted"; and Bureau of Labor Statistics, "Employee Benefits in the United Sates 1993–94," by Ann C. Foster. *Compensation and Working Conditions On Line*, Spring, 1977, Vol. 2, No. 1. Both are found at <www.bls.gov>

3. See the New Party's Web Site, <www.newparty.org>, for information on living-wage campaigns.

4. M. Weisbrot, and M.Sforza-Roderick. *Baltimore's Living Wage Law: An Analysis of the Fiscal and Economic Costs of Baltimore City Ordinance 442*. The Preamble Center for Public Policy, 1997, <www.preamble.org>

5. Jenn Kern. Interview, April 7, 1998.

6. Kern.

7. New Party, op. cit.

8. Kern, see note 5 above.

9. Kern.

10. Kern.

11. Kern.

12. Kern.

13. R. Nixon. "Horses and High Tech," *Southern Exposure*, Fall, 1994.

14. Ibid.

15. Ibid.

16. Louisiana Department of Environmental Quality. *Louisiana Environment Tax Scorecard*. State of Louisiana, 1990.

17. Rosalinda Palacios. Interview, April 29, 1998.

18. Palacios.

19. Palacios.

20. Amos White. Interview, April 23, 1998

21. Palacios, see note 17 above.

22. Amos White. *The Kids First! Initiative: A Guide to How One Community Successfully Campaigned for Funding for Children & Youth Services in Oakland*. Kids First! Coalition, Oakland, CA, 1998.

23. Palacios, see note 17 above.

24. White, see note 19 above.

25. Palacios, see note 17 above.

CHAPTER 4

1. Martin Luther King, Jr. "Black Power Defined," originally in *New York Times Magazine*, June 11, 1967 and published in *I Have A Dream: Writings and Speeches that Changed the World* (James M. Washington, ed.), Harper San Francisco, 1986. p. 154.

2. Colleen Floyd-Carroll. Interview, April 14, 1998.

3. Serena Chen. Interview, March 15, 1998.

4. R. Nixon. "Strip-mining neighbor gives SLAPP in the face," *Roanoke Times*, February 16, 1998.

5. Greg Akili. Interview, February 11, 1997.

6. Frederick Douglass. *Life and Times of Frederick Douglass*, Crowell-Collier Publishing Company, New York, 1962. p. 481.

7. Solomon Rivera. Interview, April 5, 1998.

8. Rivera.

9. Floyd-Carroll, see note 2 above.

10. Taj James. Interview, April 5, 1998.

11. James.

12. James.

13. Thandi Hicks-Harper. Interview, February 12, 1997.

CHAPTER 5

1. Quoted in Carter Harris. "President George Clinton on the State of the Funk Nation," *Pulse* Magazine, MTS, Inc., August, 1994. p.4.

2. Gil Scott Heron. "The Revolution Will Not Be Televised," on *The Revolution Will Not Be Televised*, Flying Dutchman Productions, RCA Records, lyrics by G.S. Heron, 1974.

3. Roger Lewis. *Outlaws of America, The Underground Press and Its Context: Notes on a Cultural Revolution.* Penguin Books, 1972. p. 19.

4. Ben Bagdikian. *The Media Monopoly.* Beacon Press, Boston, 1992. p.72.

5. R. McChesney. *Corporate Media and the Threat to Democracy.* Seven Stories Press, New York. 1997.

6. David Croteau and William Hoynes. *By Invitation Only: How the Media Limit Public Debate.* Common Courage, Monroe, ME, 1994.

7. Ibid.

8. McChesney. op. cit., p. 7.

9. Lori Dorfman. Interview, February 22, 1999.

10. Charlotte Ryan. *Prime Time Activism.* South End Press, Boston, 1991. p. 55.

11. Shanto Iyengaar. *Is Anyone Responsible? How Television Frames Political Issues.* Chicago University Press, Chicago,1991.

12. Ibid.

13. A more complete discussion of the concepts in this section are found in Lawrence Wallack, et al. *Media Advocacy and Public Health: Power for Prevention.* Sage Publications. 1993.

14. Erna Smith. *What Color is the News?* Center for the Integration and Improvement of Journalism, San Francisco State University, 1992.

15. Charyn Sutton. Interview, January 23, 1993.

16. See Note 14 and Farai Chideya. *Don't Believe the Hype.* Penguin Books, 1995.

17. See Iyengaar, op. cit.; also, F. D. Gilliam, S. Iyengaar, A. Simon, and O. Wright. "Crime in Black and White: The Violent, Scary World of Local News," in S. Iyengaar and R. Reeves, eds. *Do the Media Govern? Politicians, Voters, and Reporters in America.* Sage Publications, 1997.

18. Fred Ross, Sr. *Axioms for Organizers* (pamphlet). Neighbor to Neighbor Education Fund, San Francisco, 1989. p. 17.

CHAPTER 6

1. Lewis Carroll. *Alice's Adventures in Wonderland.* World Publishing Company, Cleveland, OH, 1946. p.127.

2. Phil Kuntz. "Alcohol Beverage Industry Lobbies for Bill to Gut Substance Abuse Agency Seen as Threat," *Wall Street Journal,* August 14, 1995.

3. Ibid.

4. Ibid.

5. Anonymous interview subject. Interview, October 15, 1995.

6. Anonymous interview subject. Interview, April 18, 1997.

7. Philip J. Hilts. "Law on Access to Research Data Pleases Business, Alarms Science," *New York Times*, July 31, 1999, p.1

8. Data calculated from Contra Costa County election results and campaign committee financial reports filed in November 1991, Registrar of Voters.

9. National Friends of the Bus Riders Union. *Letter to Constance Rice*, July 15, 1997.

10. Jason DeParle. "Shrinking the Welfare Rolls Leaves Record High Share of Minorities," *New York Times*, July 26, 1999, p.1.

11. See Susan Faludi. *Backlash*. Crown Publishing, New York, 1991.

12. The Women's Budget of the Women's International League for Peace and Freedom can be found at <www.feminist.org>

13. Taj James. Interview, August 2, 1999.

14. See the Feminist Majority Foundation website at <www.feminist.org> for more information on the Wal-Mart campaign and other initiatives to expand reproductive health care.

15. Berkeley Media Studies Group. *Analyzing News on Affirmative Action: Executive Summary*. Berkeley, 1998.

Useful Books

TRAINING & ORGANIZING

K. Bobo, J. Kendall, and S. Max. *Organizing for Social Change: A Manual for Activists in the 1990s.* Seven Locks Press, Arlington, VA 22210, 1990. (800) 354-5348.

Anne Hope and Sally Timmel. *Training for transformation: a handbook for community workers.* Mambo Press, Gweru, Zimbabwe, 1984. Out of print, but copies are often available through <www.amazon.com> special order services.

J. P. Kretzmann, and J. L. McKnight. *Building Communities from the Inside Out: A Path Toward Mobilizing a Community's Assets.* ACTA Publications, Chicago, 1993. (800) 397-2282.

R. Arnold, et al. *Educating for a Change.* Doris Miller Institute, Toronto, 1991. Out of print.

SOCIO-ECONOMIC & POLITICAL ANALYSIS

David Korten. *When Corporations Rule the World.* Kumarian Press, West Hartford, CT, 1995. (203) 953-0214.

William Leach. *Land of Desire: Merchants, Power and the Rise of a New American Culture.* Vintage Books, 1993.

James Scotts. *Domination and the Arts of Resistance: Hidden Transcripts.* Yale University Press, 1990.

Holly Sklar. *Chaos or Community? Seeking Solutions, Not Scapegoats for Bad Economics.* South End Press, 1995.

MEDIA

D. Hazen and J. Winokur, eds. *We the Media: A Citizens' Guide to Fighting for Media Democracy.* New Press, New York, 1997.

Shanto Iyengaar. *Is Anyone Responsible? How Television Frames Political Issues.* Chicago University Press, 1991.

Lawrence Wallack, et al. *Media Advocacy and Public Health: Power for Prevention.* Sage Publications,1993.

Lawrence Wallack, et al. *News for a Change: An Advocate's Guide to Working with the Media.* Sage Publications, 1999.

Resources

CONTACT INFORMATION FOR CASE STUDY PROFILES

Association of Community Organizations for Reform Now (ACORN)
739 8th Street, SE
Washington, DC 20003
(202) 547-2500 (voice) • (202) 546-2483 (fax)
dcnatacorn@acorn.org (e-mail)
www.acorn.org/community (website)

Californians for Justice
1611 Telegraph Avenue, Suite 206
Oakland, CA 94612
(510) 452-2728 (voice) • (510) 452-3552 (fax)
caljustice@igc.org (e-mail)
www.igc.apc.org/cfj (website)

Community Coalition for Substance Abuse Prevention and Treatment
8101 S. Vermont Avenue
Los Angeles, CA 90044
(213) 750-9087 (voice) • (213) 750-9640 (fax)
www.ccsapt.org (website)

Baltimore Citywide Liquor Coalition for Better Rules and Regulations
218 W. Saratoga Street, 4th Floor
Baltimore, MD 21201
(410) 539-1369 (voice) • (410) 539-7895 (fax)
cacasciani@msn.com (e-mail)
www.cpha.baltimore.org (website)

Louisiana Coalition for Tax Justice
8841 Blue Bonnet Boulevard
Baton Rouge, LA 70810
(504) 923-3106 (voice) • (504) 923-3144 (fax)
taxwar@aol.com (e-mail)
http://members.aol.com/taxwar/lcindex.html (website)

Kids First! Coalition
2025 E. 12th Street
Oakland, CA 94606
(510) 533-1092 (voice) • (510) 533-6825 (fax)
kidsfirst@lanminds.com (e-mail)
www.ebayc.org (website)

MEDIA

Berkley Media Studies Group
2140 Shattuck Avenue, Suite 804
Berkeley, CA 94704
(510) 204-9700 (voice) • (510) 204-9710 (fax)
woodruff@bsmg.org (e-mail)

Fairness and Accuracy in Reporting (FAIR)
130 W. 25th Street
New York, NY 10001
(212) 633-6700 (voice) • (212) 727-7668 (fax)
fair@fair.org (e-mail)
www.fair.org (website)

We Interrupt this Message
965 Mission Street, Suite 220
San Francisco, CA 94103
(415) 537-9437 (voice) • (415) 537-9439 (fax)
interrupt@igc.org (e-mail)

YOUTH ORGANIZING

Tobacco Industry Gets Hammered by Teens (TIGHT)
Colleen Floyd-Carroll
Community Wellness & Prevention Program
Contra Costa Health Services
597 Center Avenue
Martinez, CA 94553
(626) 313-6834 (voice)

Billo Communications
Dr. Thandi Hicks-Harper
4511 Cedell Place
Temple Hills, MD 20748
(301) 899-7187 (voice) • (301) 899-7189 (fax)
williedell@aol.com (e-mail)

Coleman Youth Advocates
Taj James
2601 Mission Street
San Francisco, CA 94110
(415) 641-4362 (voice) • (415) 641-1708 (fax)
coleman@sirius.com (e-mail)

LISTEN, Inc.
Lisa Sullivan
1436 U Street, NW, Suite 201
Washington, D. C.20009
(202) 483-4494 (voice)
www.lisn.org (website)

COMMUNITY DEVELOPMENT AND ORGANIZING

The Asset-Based Community Development Institute
Institute for Policy Research
Northwestern University
2040 Sheridan Rd
Evanston, IL 60208
(847) 491-3518 (voice) • (847) 491-9916 (fax)
e-walsh@nwu.edu (e-mail)
www.nwu.edu/IPR/abcd.html (website)

Center for Community Change
100 Wisconsin Ave, NW
Washington, DC 20007
(202) 342-0567 (voice) • (202) 333-5462 (fax)
www.commchange.org (website)

Center for Regional and Neighborhood Action
720 Franklin Street
Denver, CO 80218
(303) 477-9985 (voice) • (303) 477-9986 (fax)

Center for Third World Organizing
1218 E. 21st Street
Oakland, CA 94606
(510) 533-7583 (voice) • (510) 533-0923 (fax)
ctwo@sirius.com (e-mail)
www.ctwo.org (website)

Community Development Institute
321 Bell Street
East Palo Alto, CA 94303
(650) 327-5846 (voice) • (650) 327-4430 (fax)

Midwest Academy
225 W. Ohio Street, Suite 250
Chicago, IL 60610
312-645-6010 (voice) • 312-645-6018 (fax)
76065.1637@compuserve.com (e-mail)

National Civic League
1445 Market Street, Suite 300
Denver, CO 80202
(303) 571-4343 (voice)
www.csn.net/ncl (website)

TECHNICAL ASSISTANCE AND MODEL POLICIES

Advocacy Institute
1707 L Street, NW, Suite 400
Washington, DC 20012
(202) 659-8475 (voice) • (202) 659-8484 (fax)
info@advocacy.org (e-mail)
www.advocacy.org (website)

Americans for Nonsmokers' Rights
2530 San Pablo Avenue, Suite J
Berkeley, CA 94702
(510) 841-3032 (voice) • (510) 841-7702 (fax)
anr@no-smoke.org (e-mail)
www.no-smoke.org (website)

Applied Research Center
3781 Broadway
Oakland, CA 94609
(510) 653-3415 (voice) • (510) 653-3427 (fax)
arc@arc.org (e-mail) • www.arc.org (website)

Californians for Responsible Gun Laws
2140 Shattuck Avenue, Suite 1201
Berkeley, CA 94704
(510) 649-8946 (voice) • (510) 649-7894 (fax)

Center For Policy Alternatives
1875 Connecticut Avenue, NW, Suite 710
Washington, DC 20009
(202) 387-6030 (voice) • (202) 986-2539 (fax)
info@cfpa.org (e-mail) • www.cfpa.org (website)

Communities Concerned About Corporations
5104 42nd Avenue
Hyattsville, MD 20781
(301) 779-1000 (voice) • (301) 779-1001 (fax)

Legal Environmental Assistance Foundation (LEAF)
1115 North Gadsden Street
Tallahassee, FL 32303
(850) 681-2591 (voice) • (850) 224-1275 (fax)
leaf@lewisweb.net (e-mail)
www.ficus.usf.edu/orgs/leaf (website)

Preamble Collaborative
1737 21st Street, NW
Washington, DC 20009
(202) 265-3263 (voice) • (202) 265-3647 (fax)
preamble@rtk.net (e-mail)

Working Group on Community Right to Know
US PIRG Education Fund
218 D Street, NW
Washington, DC 20003
(202) 544-9586 (voice) • (202) 546-2461 (fax)
orum@rtk.net (e-mail)
www.rtk.net/wcs (website)

Index

Surveys, 82, 89
  examples of in campaigns, 30, 72
Sutton, Charyn, 134
Synergy, 119

Target, 129–30
  and accountability sessions, 103
  changing to more vulnerable, 95
  clear, 83
  decision making process of, 96
  identifying a, 94–6
  more receptive to industry interests, 101
  strengths & weaknesses, 95
Tax-exempt status & advocacy, 144
Tax reductions to businesses, 66–9
Telecommunications Act, 139
Testing the waters, 113–4
Thematic stories, 125–6, 128
Think tanks See Policy analysis organizations
Thomas, Bev, 41, 42, 43–4, 48–50, 51
Three strikes criminal justice initiative, 106
TIGHT (Tobacco Industry Gets Hammered by Teens), 108
Tobacco See also Tobacco control; Headings
  beginning with alcohol & tobacco
  grassroots efforts to reduce availability, 1, 3, 16,
    25–54, 133–4
  social costs of, 16
Tobacco billboards See Billboards, alcohol & tobacco
Tobacco control
  & electronic media, 158
  companies settling health claims, 141
  lawsuits attacking, 149
  message, 127
  restrictions on activities, 145
Toxics March, 66, 67
Trade unions See Unions
Translation, 36–7, 105
Tulane Environmental Law Center, 149

U.S. Supreme Court, 46
Unions
  and living wage campaigns, 56, 57, 60, 63, 64
  and Kids First! Campaign, 76
Uptown cigarette campaign, Philadelphia, 85, 133–4
Urban League See Baltimore Urban League

Validating people's perceptions, 23–4
Values
  community, 83
  family, 152
  guiding, 140–1
  progressive, 7
  shared, 138
Victims, 135
  with standing, 92
Victory, defense of, 115
  defining, 84
Violence Prevention Initiative (VPI), 123–4
Violence, and youth, 72

Vision, 82, 83–4, 134
  possibility of achieving, 159
  statement, 83, 122–3
Visuals, developing compelling, 127
Voluntary agreements, 91–2
Volunteeers, attracting and using, 83, 97–100
Volunteer base, shrinking, 111
Voter registration & tracking, 156–7
Voter turnout, low, 147, 156

Wages, 3, 15, 61
Walkabout, 89
Wal-Mart, 153–4
Walters, Rita, 33
War on drugs, 30
War on Poverty, 5–6
Wealth-fare See Tax reductions to businesses
Websites, 139
We Interrupt This Message, 137
Welfare, 125, 126, 151
Welfare Rights Organization, National (NWRO), 60
Welfare-to-work See Workfare
West Coast Publishers' Association, 130–1
White, Amos, 74
Williams, Aaron, 109
Williams, Alberta Tinsley, 131
Winnable issue, 83
Women's Budget, 153
Women's International League of Peace & Freedom, 153
Women's movement, reforms by under attack,
  150, 152–4
Woo, Mike, 34
Workers See Living-wage campaigns
Workfare, 64–5
Working Partnerships USA, 57
WRIST test, 83

X brand cigarette campaign, Boston, 85, 130

Y-MAC, 108–10,
Youth
  advocacy groups, 74, 77
  and drug trade, 70–1
  appeal of deadly products to, 85
  culture, 110–11
  development, 69, 72–3, 77–8
  investment in developing, 71
  involvement, support services for, 107–8
  leadership, 105–7
  mentoring of, 107, 109
  organizing, 105–11
  political education of, 108
  punishing, 69, 71, 72
  research & analysis by, 107
  services, spending cuts, 105
Youth Making A Change See Y-MAC

Zoning law discrimination, 26

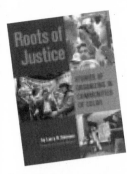

ORDER HERE

(Subscribe to the *Grassroots Fundraising Journal* separately in box below.)

TITLE	ITEM NUMBER	UNIT PRICE	QUANTITY	TOTAL
	___ ___ - __ __ __ __			
	___ ___ - __ __ __ __			
	___ ___ - __ __ __ __			
	___ ___ - __ __ __ __			
	___ ___ - __ __ __ __			
	___ ___ - __ __ __ __			
	___ ___ - __ __ __ __			
			SUBTOTAL	

TAKE A DISCOUNT: 5–9 copies of any one title: take **20%** off that title's total
10 or more copies of any one title: take **40%** off that title's total

less discount

TOTAL

SUBSCRIBE TO THE
GRASSROOTS FUNDRAISING JOURNAL

United States
☐ 1 year @ $32 _____
☐ 2 years @ $58 _____

Canada, Mexico and Overseas
☐ 1 year @ $39 _____
☐ 2 years @ $65 _____

Please allow 6 weeks for new subscriptions. There are no tax or shipping charges for subscriptions.

☐ **Please send me a free Chardon Press Catalog.**

CREDIT CARD ORDERS

☐ MasterCard ☐ Visa ☐ Discover ☐ Amex
Card #: _____
Exp. date: _____
Signature: _____

SHIPPING & HANDLING CHARGES

ORDER TOTALS	SHIPPING FEE
$ 5.00 – 10.00	**$ 2.00**
$ 10.01 – 25.00	**$ 4.00**
$ 25.01 – 50.00	**$ 6.00**
$ 50.01 – 75.00	**$ 8.00**
$ 75.01 –100.00	**$10.00**
$100.01 or more	**10% of order**

Books normally shipped bookrate; large orders shipped UPS Ground. Please allow 2–4 weeks for delivery.

☐ 3 Day Select . . . . fee at left × 2
☐ 2nd Day Air . . . . fee at left × 3
☐ Overnight . . . . fee at left × 4
☐ Priority Mail flat
(single book order only) $5
☐ International Air Mail
(including Canada & Mexico) . . . fee at left × 2
Payment in U.S. dollars only.

TOTAL YOUR ORDER HERE

Subtotal from ***ORDER HERE*** box $ _____
In CA add 8.25% sales tax $ _____
Shipping & Handling (see chart above) $ _____
Grassroots Fundraising Journal Subscription $ _____
TOTAL AMOUNT ENCLOSED: $ _____

Name _____
Organization _____
Address _____
City / State / Zip _____
If we have questions about your order, should we reach you by:
☐ Phone _____ OR ☐ E-mail _____

PAYABLE TO CHARDON PRESS: 3781 Broadway • Oakland, CA 94611
PHONE: (888) 458-8588 • IN SF BAY AREA: (510) 596-8160 • FAX: (510) 596-8822 • E-MAIL: chardon@chardonpress.com
www.chardonpress.com